BLACK CHURCH WHITE CONVENTION

"Mark Johnson offers a practical resource that can be utilized by a congregation or an individual to move beyond the noise and rhetoric that overshadows the path to racial reconciliation in the SBC. His in-depth research of the complicated history of the SBC brings into focus an ever progressing movement toward one reconciled body of believers in Jesus Christ our Lord."

—**Leroy Fountain**, church health consultant,
New Orleans Baptist Association and church
planter consultant, North American Mission Board, and
Carolyn Fountain, SBC executive committee member

"Mark Louis Johnson, Sr. reflects on a decade old journey as a pastor of a black, urban church in Cleveland, OH, navigating its reluctance to affiliate with the Southern Baptist Convention (SBC). By combining historical documents with relational intentionality, this book reveals both missed opportunities and intentional efforts toward racial reconciliation. *Black Church White Convention* is a timely, user friendly, and must-read bookshelf addition for ones who seek to understand SBC's potential Great Commission legacy among not only people of color but also among all who profess Jesus Christ as Lord and Savior and who seek unity in racial reconciliation."

—**Carolyn E. Gordon**, PhD, former member
of Liberty Hill Baptist Church

"Mark Johnson challenges believers to seek true unity in Christ by sharing with us his journey of leading his church to embrace unity across racial and cultural barriers. The poignant account of their journey will speak to all believers as we strive to become congregations that look more like Heaven as we come together from every tribe and background. May we all embrace this call to be unified as believers in the local church and denominations in order to reach all people with the gospel of Jesus Christ."

—**Teman Knight**, senior pastor, Heritage
Baptist Church, Montgomery, AL

"In these pages, Mark Louis Johnson Sr. courageously tackles the complex issues surrounding the divide between black and white churches. Mark shares his personal journey and insights, highlighting the power of faith, understanding, and unity. As you read, I hope it inspires you to reflect on your own experiences and encourages you to take bold steps toward building connections across cultural lines. This book is not just a call to action; it's an invitation to be part of a transformative journey toward togetherness."

—**Kevin Lichfield**, associational missionary of the Santee Baptist Association, Sumter, SC

"*Black Church, White Convention* by Mark Johnson is a must-read for all Christians, particularly those who identify as Southern Baptists. It tells the encouraging story of a young pastor leading his Black church family to confront old wounds and reconsider their relationship with the Southern Baptist Convention. Mark guides an understandably reluctant congregation through the SBC's historical resolutions, revealing its often awkward attempts to align with Scripture in its views and attitudes toward African American brothers and sisters. Through this process, a spirit of grace emerges, leading to a renewed commitment to the Great Commission. This is gospel-centered racial reconciliation at its best."

—**Ed Litton**, senior pastor, Redemption Church, former president of the Southern Baptist Convention

"Dr. Mark Johnson's story of explaining the experience of a Black church in a predominantly White convention to the Liberty Hill Baptist Church congregation in Cleveland resonates with a similar conversation I had with the congregation of Franklin Avenue Baptist Church in New Orleans about being part of the Southern Baptist Convention. This insightful and informative book is a must-read for any Christian interested in racial reconciliation, unity, and hope, especially within the context of a Black church in a White convention."

—**Fred Luter Jr.**, senior pastor, Franklin Avenue Baptist Church, New Orleans, former president of the Southern Baptist Convention

BLACK CHURCH WHITE CONVENTION

A PASTOR'S STORY OF HOPE

MARK LOUIS JOHNSON SR.

ACADEMIC®
BRENTWOOD, TENNESSEE

Black Church, White Convention: A Pastor's Story of Hope

Published by B&H Academic®
Brentwood, Tennessee

ISBN: 978-1-4300-8840-0

Dewey Decimal Classification: 305.8
Subject Heading: BLACK BAPTISTS \ BLACK CHURCHES \ RACE RELATIONS

The web addresses referenced in this book were live and correct at the time of the book's publication but may be subject to change.

Information in this book quoting historical SBC Resolutions is taken from "Resources in Resolutions," https://www.sbc.net/resource-library/resolutions/.

Cover design by Gearbox. Cover image by Shutterstock

Printed in the United States of America
30 29 28 27 26 25 VP 1 2 3 4 5 6 7 8 9 10

CONTENTS

ACKNOWLEDGMENTS

I would like to express my deepest gratitude to my beloved family, especially my wife Heather and our children Mark Jr., Jonathan, Victoria, and Benjamin. Your unwavering support and understanding have been the cornerstone of my journey. Your presence has turned every twist and turn into an adventure, and I am endlessly thankful for each moment we have shared together.

To the Liberty Hill Baptist Church community, thank you for your willingness to embark on an incredible journey. Together, we have changed lives, and I am profoundly grateful for our time together.

A special and heartfelt gratitude to my former director of missions, Kevin Litchfield, and all the pastors and leaders of the Cleveland Hope Association in Cleveland, Ohio. Your remarkable partnerships have transformed lives, planted churches, provided essential training, and opened doors to limitless possibilities for unity within the body of Christ, advancing the kingdom of God. While there is always room for growth, together, we moved the needle.

INTRODUCTION

As a third-generation pastor, sitting in hospital rooms as people stared at death became a place of familiarity. I grew up captivated by the calm demeanor of my father and grandfather as they held hands, listened to stories, and provided the "ministry of presence" for parishioners in their time of need. From my nine-year-old perspective, reading Scriptures, singing hymns, or reciting the Lord's Prayer seemed to bring mostly solace to those transitioning from this life to eternal life with Christ. However, entering my seventh year as the eighth senior pastor of the Liberty Hill Baptist Church in Cleveland, Ohio, something felt different the day I walked into that familiar setting. An uneasiness settled in my heart as I approached the bedside of a parishioner who would soon no longer feel a cool breeze on her face. As I entered that hospital room, my hunch became a reality. "Pastor Grandson," the name used by some parishioners to express the generation gap between the pulpit and the pew, became the invisible barrier for discussing certain topics. I would soon find out that race was one of those topics.

Initially cordial, her demeanor changed when she said, "Pastor, I do not want you to do my eulogy!" Having heard hundreds of requests throughout my thirty years of ministry, this request escaped all my theological training courses at Princeton and New Orleans Seminary. With a blank stare in her eyes, she shared her frustration with our black church joining a white convention. After I absorbed that gut punch, she revealed a seminal incident from her childhood that, understandably, lingered years later: the lynching of her elementary school principal. Hearing the horrid details explained the source of her pain, and the impact of that trauma was unmistakable. However, it appeared that a weight lifted as she made known to me her sentiments. I knew there was a cost for pursuing racial unity, but I did not expect it to come this way. I then wondered, how many other eulogies I would forego in pursuit of racial harmony?

As a product of the civil rights movement, my experience of being bused from an all-black school to an all-white school came with its own set of challenges. Yet in retrospect, that busing experience played a pivotal role in allowing my parents to shape a biblical worldview that underscored the desire to pursue unity. My parents, Henry and Kathy Johnson, exemplified a life of faith that taught the value of the *imago dei*—a principle I still uphold. Although generations removed from slavery, Reconstruction, and the civil rights movement, as "Pastor Grandson," I had to acknowledge the diverse generational perspectives among Liberty Hill parishioners. I knew generalizing their views could be seen as insensitive and oversimplify a complex reality. However, my pursuit of racial unity paled in comparison to my desire to see people of all races experiencing new life in Christ.

The Beginning

"That racist organization?" were the resolute words of an influential parishioner at the predominantly black Liberty Hill Baptist Church in Cleveland, Ohio, during the vote on whether to join the predominantly white Southern Baptist Convention (SBC). Despite our church having hosted hundreds of Southern Baptist missionaries the previous summer, the opposition to joining "that racist organization" seemed insurmountable. Memories of times past resurfaced as parishioners, some of whom had moved north in search of a better life, shared impassioned stories of racial tensions, intimidation tactics, and even death tolls. A longtime parishioner of Liberty Hill shared the details of the lynching of her elementary school principal, whose body hung from a tree outside her school building. This vivid recollection represented the resolute hearts of many parishioners struggling with rewriting Liberty Hill's history to include a convention with an oppressive past. The decision to join the SBC was met with deep-seated concerns rooted in historical traumas and fear of aligning with an organization perceived as perpetuating racial injustice. Moderating parishioners' uneasiness meant answering the one-word question in hearts and minds: Why? Beneath that one-word question lay a comfortable life rhythm unwilling to go quietly into the night. The change meant a disruption from the standard patterns of life that allowed the black church to remain appropriately segregated. However, over an eight-year period, the black church/white convention union would add historical firsts to Liberty Hill's history and cause an awakening in the Cleveland community that expanded the kingdom of God.

The Black Church

Initially referred to as a "mission" formed by a group of baptized believers on September 22, 1917, Liberty Hill Baptist Church held its first meetings in homes before renting a space in Cleveland, Ohio, for fifty dollars a month. On July 10, 1918, the mission became fully organized and received its official name. Despite being small initially, Liberty Hill experienced significant growth, with membership reaching two thousand by the mid 1950s.[1] As the church continued to grow, the leadership faced the decision of whether to build a new facility or purchase an existing property. The answer came in the form of a massive Jewish Synagogue in Cleveland's East Side area, known as Hough (pronounced huff). This acquisition provided the necessary space to accommodate the increasing number of parishioners.

Liberty Hill's prominence in the 1950s marked a proud moment of independence for an African American church striving to have its concerns taken seriously by city officials. With well over one thousand members, a church of this size could mobilize, create wealth, and demand political attention amidst the rise of social injustices. Black churches nationwide served as advocates for African American communities, and leaders of Liberty Hill became that voice amid swelling racial tensions. The 1950s marked a significant shift in Cleveland's landscape due to the flight of middle-class Caucasians and the influx of working-class African Americans. The Hough area, containing a population of sixty-six thousand, comprised 90 percent

---

[1] Steven Nguyen, Cleveland Historical Society, "Euclid Avenue Temple: Anshe Chesed Congregation of Cleveland." Cleveland Historical, December 13, 2020, https://clevelandhistorical.org/items/show/924.

African American,[2] reflected the demographic changes and challenges faced by urban communities during that period.

African American residents expressed concerns about various issues, including segregated schools, dilapidated housing, dysfunctional community recreation centers, unemployment, the lack of garbage collection, and racial profiling by law enforcement officers. The Cleveland Police Department, under the leadership of Romanian-born Mayor Ralph S. Locher, faced criticism for racially profiling, brutalizing, harassing, and neglecting the needs of the African American community. The lack of response to the concerns raised by African Americans led to protests, which Mayor Locher largely dismissed, expecting them to fade away, especially during the harsh winter season. However, Mayor Locher underestimated the persistence of the nine-month protest in 1966 and its impact on the city of Cleveland. Racially charged events permeated the city, contributing to the widening divide between African Americans and Caucasians. The protests underscored the deep-seated issues and tensions within the community that needed to be addressed.

The "us versus them" mentality began to take root as African Americans grappled with the harsh realities of discrimination. Small racial encounters started to crack the proverbial bow, causing it to break and leading to what became known as the "Hough Riots," which resulted in four slain African Americans, fifty injured citizens, and 275 arrests, as well as robberies, vandalism, arson, looting, and the calling of the National Guard. The Hough Riots,

---

[2] Richard Raponi, "The Hough Uprisings of 1966," Cleveland Historical, Sep 12, 2010, https://clevelandhistorical.org/items/show/7.

lasting from July 18 to July 23, 1966, set the Hough community ablaze, occurring just two blocks from Liberty Hill Baptist Church.[3] While the church itself was undamaged, the impact on the psyche of parishioners remained immeasurable.

Liberty Hill, like many African American churches in Cleveland, played a crucial role in the recovery of the Hough neighborhood. However, the lack of diversity in the Hough area posed a challenge to addressing race relations. Redlining, a financial services discriminatory practice against neighborhoods with a significant number of racial or ethnic minorities, along with the departure of black-owned businesses and white middle-class families, had a significant impact on the Hough area, depleting the community of its resources. Churches in the area stepped in to provide spiritual support, educational assistance, food banks, clothing pantries, and other community events to aid in the recovery process. However, the pressing need for racial reconciliation often took a back seat as the community focused on survival.

The White Convention

Before the formation of the Southern Baptist Convention in 1845, the Triennial Convention, established in 1814, served as the first national Baptist organization in the United States.[4] Originally named the General Missionary Convention of the Baptist Denomination in the United States for Foreign Missions, this

---

[3] Raponi.

[4] Jesse C. Fletcher, *Southern Baptist Convention: A Sesquicentennial History* (Nashville: B&H, 1994), 35.

organization brought together Baptist churches from Northern and Southern cities with the shared mission of making disciples of all nations. Despite the Northern and Southern churches unifying over missions, the issue of slavery revealed underlying instability that cast a shadow over the perceived inseparability of Baptists.

The Emancipation Act of 1833 in the United Kingdom, just twelve years before the split of the Triennial Convention leading to the formation of the Southern Baptist Convention, marked the abolition of slavery in the British Empire.[5] Baptists in England sent a letter encouraging their counterparts in the American colonies to follow suit.[6] However, the economic and political systems established after the Revolutionary War were deeply rooted in the monetary value of African lives. Theological differences on the issue of slavery led to disunity, dysfunction, and death, proving consequential in shaping young America. While other religious groups in the late eighteenth and early nineteenth centuries, such as Mennonites, Quakers, German Pietists, and Congregationalists, supported the abolition of slavery in the American colonies, Baptists in America maintained a policy of noninterference in civil affairs.[7] Although some associations within the Triennial Convention responded, with the Ketockton Primitive Baptist Association of Virginia proposing a plan of gradual emancipation in 1787, the matter was eventually

[5] Fletcher, 36.

[6] Fletcher, 36.

[7] Robert G. Torbet, *A History of the Baptists* (Valley Forge, PA: Judson, 1963), 282.

dropped.[8] However, statesman and minister John Leland argued that being a minister of the gospel did not preclude being a vocal citizen and influential statesman.[9]

John Leland presented a resolution to the Baptist General Committee in 1789, advocating for the gradual abolishment of slavery.[10] However, the following year, the association claimed a lack of clarity about the resolution, leaving the issue to each autonomous church.[11] This decision allowed enslavers to advise without being held accountable for the treatment of enslaved people. While some autonomous churches formed emancipation parties with abolitionist preachers, most Baptists remained cautious about the issue of slavery, guided by a hesitancy to interfere in civil affairs.[12] As the nation expanded, the issue of slavery created a growing divide within the Triennial Convention between Northern and Southern churches.[13] The decision not to send missionary candidates overseas who were slaveholders further exacerbated the tensions, leading officials from Baptist churches in the South gathered in Augusta, Georgia (1845), to form the SBC.[14]

---

[8] Torbet, 282.

[9] Torbet, 283.

[10] Noah Breyman, "The Life of John Leland: Statesman," The Ethics & Religious Liberty Commission of the Southern Baptist Convention, May 14, 2014, https://erlc.com/resource-library/articles/the-life-of-john-leland-statesman/.

[11] Breyman.

[12] Breyman.

[13] Jarvis J. Williams and Kevin M. Jones, *Removing the Stain of Racism from the Southern Baptist Convention: Diverse African American and White Perspectives* (Nashville: B&H Academic, 2017), 61.

[14] Fletcher, *Southern Baptist Convention*, 40.

The Connection

In 1956, the parishioners of Liberty Hill Baptist Church purchased a massive Jewish synagogue from the Anshe Chesed congregation. This synagogue, equipped with a 1,000-seat sanctuary, a 1,000-seat theater, 25 classrooms, a 450-seat dining hall, and a commercial kitchen, played a crucial role in helping its surrounding Hough community.[15] In 2009, I became the pastor of Liberty Hill Baptist Church and continued the work of my predecessor in transforming the community by seeking partnerships with like-minded people and organizations. Though I faced numerous rejections in the search for partnerships, a phone call to an organization called Cleveland Hope proved to be a turning point, as their director of missions responded positively and opened doors to nationwide partnerships within the SBC.

Cleveland Hope, as a local association of the SBC, played a crucial role by providing training, fellowship, and support, as well as increased awareness of and participation in local, state, and worldwide missions. Despite my initial lack of knowledge about the SBC, my friendship with the director of missions (Kevin Litchfield) flourished because of a shared commitment to God and love for all people. This friendship led to fruitful collaborations, including multicultural worship services, leadership training sessions, regional workshops, mission trips, retreats, pastoral outings, community carnivals, international missions, and various

---

[15] "Negro Church Buys Temple at Euclid—82," *Cleveland Plain Dealer*, January 27, 1956.

fellowships. The relationships formed extended beyond racial lines to include diverse churches such as Ukrainian, Hispanic, Bhutanese, and Egyptian churches, churches of the deaf, and others in the region. Recognizing the success of this collaboration, Cleveland Hope eventually relocated its headquarters to Liberty Hill Baptist Church. However, despite the positive transformations, I noted that a sense of cordiality and niceness seemed to linger in the atmosphere. I sensed a caution that permeated the atmosphere as Liberty Hill members engaged with white Southern Baptist missionaries. Despite multiple activities bringing diverse groups together, there was a clear uneasiness associated with the unspoken pain of the past. Conversations with Liberty Hill leaders reflected the history of the Black Migration Movement, emphasizing a "comfort with our own people."

Moreover, some parishioners harbored hurt, distrust, anger, and unforgiveness because of past experiences with white Southerners. Despite great moments of worship and fellowship, the presence of white people awakened suppressed memories for some of Liberty Hill's members. I expressed the importance of not painting any group of people with a broad brush, of emphasizing the principles of individuality, and of recognizing diverse perspectives within any community, including Southern Baptists. The reference to Dr. Martin Luther King Jr.'s "content of their character" speech underlines the significance of judging individuals based on their character rather than making assumptions based on collective characteristics.[16]

---

[16] Martin Luther King Jr., *I Have a Dream*, ed. James M. Washington (New York: Harper Collins, 1991).

Though I acknowledged the vivid memories of some Liberty Hill parishioners shaped by historical experiences, my examination of the SBC became a meaningful step in seeking, understanding, and exploring possibilities for racial reconciliation.

The Charge

I arrived early at the Liberty Hill Baptist Church chapel to set up for a significant presentation educating Liberty Hill parishioners on racial reconciliation in the SBC. Despite the painful past of the SBC, I felt surprisingly calm. The room filled with anticipation as attendees eagerly awaited the results of my six-month study on racial reconciliation within the SBC. Liberty Hill parishioners deserved to hear the truth about the inescapable past that chained itself to the SBC. Notwithstanding the anticipated eye rolls, sighs, and seat shifting, I remained committed to presenting a four-week series on racial reconciliation.

After extensive research conducted through books, articles, journals, and academic projects, I decided that an examination and presentation of the convention's resolutions provided the best way to reduce the learning curve for Liberty Hill parishioners. From 1845 to 2017, 1,145 resolutions of the Southern Baptist Convention offered over thirty time-stamped resolutions for parishioners with no knowledge about the Southern Baptist Convention.[17]

---

[17] "Resolutions." Sbc.net. Accessed July 15, 2024. https://www.sbc.net/resource-library/resolutions/.

The Road Map

Black Church, White Convention documents an eight-year racial reconciliation journey, with the first three chapters highlighting a painful past. In "Chapter 1: Can We Retell the Story?" the early history of the SBC is examined through resolutions, revealing both challenges and hope for reconciliation. "Chapter 2: Can We Release the Hurt?" discusses in depth the painful history challenging the faith of parishioners, emphasizing the importance of engaging the hurt to understand commonalities for growth, and beginning steps forward. "Chapter 3: Can We Reestablish the Trust?" addresses the time needed to truly build a long-lasting relationship beyond cordiality. "Chapter 4: Can We Reduce the Noise?" considers the jeopardizing of unity after a tragic incident in 2012 involving a Cleveland police car chase and the deaths of Timothy Russel and Malissa Williams. The chapter explores challenges to reducing noise, especially in the context of events like that controversial 2015 acquittal of Cleveland Officer Brelo.

"Chapter 5: Can We Regain the Courage?" delves into the silence of the SBC during moments of societal controversy, such as the deaths of President John F. Kennedy and Dr. Martin Luther King Jr. The chapter addresses the lost and regained courage by the SBC messengers to advance reconciliation efforts. "Chapter 6: Can We Rediscover the Cross?" offers a theological perspective for reconciliation. The death, burial, and resurrection of Jesus Christ are the blueprint for reconciliation. Following Jesus's example is harder than one thinks. "Chapter 7: Can We Reclaim the Mission?" focuses on the importance of racial reconciliation and its impact on the Great Commission.

Let's begin our journey!

1

Can We Retell the Story?

Retelling the narrative of a painful history stands as a crucial element in the pursuit of racial reconciliation. It became apparent to me that the parishioners of Liberty Hill Baptist Church were not fully aware of the comprehensive history of the Southern Baptist Convention, and, in truth, many seemed indifferent. A protective mental barrier had been erected, shielding them from the pain, frustration, and rage deeply embedded in generations of suffering unimaginable atrocities. In my research into stories of racism and hate, I had a stark realization: some members of Liberty Hill had not merely heard these stories but had lived through them. It was a delicate chasm I needed to navigate with sensitivity, recognizing that probing old wounds could potentially lead to further distress and complications. Having synthesized the gathered information, I felt prepared to present the parishioners with a nuanced perspective on the SBC.

Although the researched information does not absolve the convention of its role in America's horrific past, it serves to provide valuable insights into the inner workings of the organization. The act of retelling the story meant delving into a brutal history that tore families apart, claimed innumerable lives, and diverted the course of future generations. Yet woven within this narrative were also glimpses of hope that managed to pierce through the darkness, offering a potential pathway forward. I felt a sense of obligation to commence my initial session by addressing the stark reality of 1845. Though challenging to accept and often difficult to grasp, slavery undeniably played a central role in the formation of the SBC. As I observed the faces of our parishioners absorbing the weight of my opening presentation, I could not help noticing a few eye rolls, arm folds, and head shakes, signaling their resistance to the unsettling reality that was gradually setting in, contrary to their initial expectations. If I had not addressed that elephant in the room, my credibility would have been lost, and the chance to present a case for racial reconciliation would have diminished.

The brutal history of being beaten, torn from families, raped, shot, lynched, and subjected to a multitude of unknown evils still lingers on America's soil. Confronting this harsh truth is imperative, as neglecting it means disregarding the lives of generations of people. In the face of such painful narratives, is it conceivable to contemplate racial reconciliation, forgiveness, and unity, or does retelling this kind of past inevitably draw lines? In my role as a researcher, there were moments when I had to physically distance myself from the laptop to grapple with the weight of my ancestral history. Similarly, as I took my time to process, I could sense the

Liberty Hill parishioners undergoing their own internal reckoning with my presentation that confronted them with the unvarnished truth about the SBC. Yet, another stark reality emerged—Southern Baptists had not prioritized racial reconciliation. Perhaps, in the broader context of America's urgent issues, such as the founding of states like Florida, Texas, Iowa, Wisconsin, California, and Minnesota, the focus on racial reconciliation was not considered worth the time.

As I delved into the exploration of racial reconciliation within the Southern Baptist Convention, the broader American context proved crucial. The genesis of the SBC occurred sixty-nine years after the Declaration of Independence, a period marked not only by the addition of states to the union but also by significant historical developments. In 1849, the California Gold Rush promised prosperity to those seeking a better life. Meanwhile, in 1857, the *Dred Scott v. Sandford* case, progressing from Missouri courts to the Supreme Court, declared that enslaved individuals were not citizens or entitled to protection from the federal government or the courts. Even as late as 1858, ministers expressed dismay over the fact that numerous wealthy individuals in cotton-growing regions allowed their enslaved people to remain uninformed about the fundamental tenets of Christianity.[1] Some enslavers held the belief that blacks were incapable of comprehending the gospel or improving their morals, leading to a prevailing consensus that

---

[1] Jesse C. Fletcher, *Southern Baptist Convention: A Sesquicentennial History* (Nashville: B&H, 1994), 40.

educating enslaved individuals was both perilous and costly.[2] This mindset was particularly entrenched in parts of the South, where some failed to recognize the value of providing education to those in bondage. Despite this challenging backdrop, the SBC, from its inception, actively shared the gospel and took a stance on this hotly debated issue, passing two resolutions that addressed the complexities around education and race within the broader societal context.

Before sharing the resolutions of the SBC, I took a moment to address any questions from parishioners who were still grappling with the introduction of my research. I recognized that broadening the perspectives of Liberty Hill parishioners might not radically alter their sentiments toward the SBC. However, essential to bringing the broader American context into view is the reality that other issues besides race mattered to the convention—a facet of the story that merits inclusion in the retelling. America's history, while built on slavery, encompasses cultural, political, educational, religious, and societal perspectives.

At the inaugural meeting of the SBC, a notable resolution titled **Resolution on Negros—Augusta, Georgia (1845)** joined others as the first set of resolutions presented from the messengers to the convention.[3] It remained crucial for Liberty Hill parishioners to understand that, despite the convention's tainted origin, the Southern Baptists acknowledged the role of religious education in the lives of enslaved people. I am aware that the use of religion

[2] Fletcher, 40.

[3] Southern Baptist Convention "Resolution on Negros," sbc.net, last modified 2000, https://www.sbc.net/resource-library/resolutions/resolution-on-negros/.

to control enslaved persons is a topic that elicited discussion and debate among parishioners at Liberty Hill. However, it is important to note that the existence of a Great Commission priority within the SBC planted seeds that would, over time, bear fruit and provide education needed for freedom and survival.

After introducing this opening resolution to the members of Liberty Hill, I encouraged them not to take offense at the title, assuring them that such titles would evolve and become less offensive as the years progressed. In the limited seven resolutions of the inaugural convention, the Board of Domestic Missions was tasked with "taking all prudent measures for the religious instruction of our colored population." The phrase "our colored population" sparked a side conversation with a parishioner at Liberty Hill, necessitating clarification on whether "our" implied ownership or membership. Internally, I acknowledged the problematic nature of this portion of the presentation but understood that a broader discussion was needed, as the SBC actively pursued religious education for all.

Presenting this information to the members of Liberty Hill Baptist Church opened a dialogue that I referred to as the exploration of "hows." How could Southern Baptists express a desire for religious education while still endorsing the institution of slavery? How could individuals professing love for the Lord allow such atrocities to occur in their midst? How could followers of Jesus Christ engage in degrading and abusive behavior toward those created in the image of God? These questions filled the room during my presentation, marking a crucial step in the journey of racial reconciliation: allowing the release of unanswerable questions. In a realm where Christians often claim to have answers for everything, the concept of sin can sometimes be thrown around as a universal explanation of all problems. However, standing before the members of Liberty Hill Baptist Church, I realized that they were not seeking ready-made answers but desired to articulate their own questions.

Initially, I prepared to offer an overly religious and pastoral response, feeling an obligation as the presenter to provide answers. Yet it became clear that there are no simple answers to the profound questions of the soul. Instead, my role was to create a safe environment for the release of questions—some possibly dormant for years, others sparked anew by the information I presented. Despite the perplexing "hows," it was crucial to acknowledge that the SBC's desire to provide religious instruction for African Americans did receive support, and a resolution to this effect passed at the inaugural convention, representing the less highlighted aspect of the convention's early history. During this period, slavery persisted as an active institution; yet this resolution uncovered an evangelical facet of the SBC interested in providing education and instruction for a marginalized population.

Presenting the gospel message was just the beginning. The SBC extended its reach by sending people of color on foreign missions to share the gospel—in 1849 Robert Hill was sent to Liberia by the Southern Baptist Convention.[4] This outreach demonstrated obedience to the Great Commission of Jesus Christ, emphasizing the imperative to make disciples. In those formative years, missions

[4] "African-American Missions." The Traveling Team, last modified February 11, 2015, https://www.thetravelingteam.org/articles/african-american-missions.

became a cornerstone as the SBC expanded independently of Northern churches.[5] The utilization of resources to extend the reach of the gospel showcased the sustainability of the newly formed convention and the cooperative efforts among churches. In an era long before the Wright brothers' invention of the airplane in 1903, missionaries traversed waters to spread the gospel message.

The 1845 resolution, which provided training for "our colored population," not only underscored the convention's commitment to inclusivity but also revealed the remarkable abilities and capabilities of people of color to effectively communicate the gospel of Jesus Christ. Minority missionaries such as George Liele, Lott Carey, and Robert Hill emerged as exemplary figures, illustrating the significant impact of investing in individuals from the colored population for the broader mission movement. Their stories became compelling narratives that spoke to the potential and influence of diverse voices within the SBC's missionary endeavors.

The **Resolution on Negroes—Charleston, South Carolina (1849)** played a pivotal role by resolving that "pastors would impart, to the colored population in their charge, information about African missions of the convention."[6] While Liberty Hill parishioners absorbed information about the SBC, I consistently underscored the significance of making this comprehensive history known. Accusations against the SBC as a racist organization were leveled without Liberty Hill parishioners having access

---

[5] Fletcher, *Southern Baptist Convention*, 52.

[6] "The Resolution on Negroes," sbc.net, May 1, 1849, https://www.sbc.net/resource-library/resolutions/resolution-on-negros-2/.

to the full knowledge of the convention's history. From as early as 1845, pastors, ministers, and religious educators within the SBC dedicated time to engage their colored population with the gospel message. Moreover, financial resources and other means were allocated to train colored missionaries, send them on mission trips, and equip them to fulfill the Great Commission amid the tumultuous backdrop of American history. Again, the purpose is not to justify wrongs, but to provide previously unknown information.

The presence of time-stamped resolutions, voted on by the messengers of the SBC, facilitated an unprecedented interaction between the past and the present, allowing for a more nuanced understanding of the convention's historical context. The frequency of racial resolutions within the SBC diminished over that time, with the next resolution related to racial reconciliation not emerging until 1868. In that nineteen-year gap, the landscape of America underwent dramatic transformations. Liberty Hill members, familiar with American history, were well-acquainted with the painful events of the 1860s. As I approached these topics, I took a moment to prepare Liberty Hill parishioners for the recounting of a challenging stretch in the story. At this juncture in the presentation, it felt important to illuminate America's history before delving into the subsequent relevant resolutions of the SBC.

In 1860, Abraham Lincoln's election marked a turning point in American history. However, the celebration was tempered by the secession of seven states from the union, causing an unprecedented divide that reshaped states' allegiances. Despite issuing no resolutions in 1860, the SBC grappled with the impact of these changes in the South. In 1861, J. J. Fleming of South Carolina proposed a motion resolving that a committee be appointed to recommend vital changes in the convention's constitution and minutes due to the recent formation of the Southern Confederacy. **The Resolution on Peace—Augusta, Georgia (1863)** took the form of a tribute to Confederate Lieutenant T. J. "Stonewall" Jackson, expressing gratitude for his achievements and the example he set.[7] While resolutions offering prayers for fallen Confederate soldiers could be understood given the relationships and connections within the SBC, the noticeable silence on the assassination of Abraham Lincoln in 1865 became a pattern of silence in selected moments. As I shared these historical details with Liberty Hill Baptist Church parishioners, they were not taken aback by the findings and readied themselves for the next phase of resolutions in the unfolding narrative.

After shedding light on the divisive history, I presented the **Resolution on Negros—Baltimore, Maryland (1868).** This resolution echoed the previous emphasis on the religious education of the "colored" population but took a step further in mission development. It suggested the implementation of necessary measures "to organize bodies of converted freedmen and assist them in settling as missionary churches in Africa." As I reached this point in the presentation, I noticed certain parishioners with smirks on their faces. After a brief pause, a comment was made: "It sounds like the Southern Baptist Convention is trying to round up black people and send them back to Africa." I chose

[7] "The Resolution on Peace," sbc.net, May 1, 1863, https://www.sbc.net/resource-library/resolutions/resolution-on-peace/.

not to respond directly to the comment but continued presenting the information, allowing for interpretation, and offering guidance. This resolution underscored the commitment to spreading the gospel; yet Southern Baptist leaders acknowledged that the proposed method "was deemed too expensive and contained too many contingencies for the Southern Baptist Convention to implement directly." Consequently, the responsibility for exploring such initiatives shifted to the "Foreign Mission Board for careful consideration."

Within a mere twenty-three years, the SBC solidified its standing as a viable channel for spreading the gospel of Jesus Christ. Despite the profound impact of the Civil War, Southern Baptists regrouped and directed their efforts toward reaching large groups of African Americans. **The Resolution on Negros—Baltimore, Maryland (1884)** reported a staggering "seven million African Americans within the states served by the Southern Baptist Convention."[8] Recognizing the immense need for religious instruction among this population, a structured system was deemed essential. The Home Mission Board recommended the establishment of institutes for colored preachers and deacons, facilitating further religious instruction "with the assistance of qualified and gifted pastors of Southern Baptist churches." Retelling the story involved grasping the magnitude of the resources mobilized by the SBC to strategize, train, finance, and educate religious leaders within black communities. This marked a significant chapter in the convention's

[8] "Resolution on Negros," sbc.net, May 1, 1884, https://www.sbc.net/resource-library/resolutions/resolution-on-negros-4/.

commitment to extending religious education and outreach beyond racial divides.

Two years following the Home Mission Board's recommendation, the **Resolution on Negroes—Montgomery, Alabama (1886)** put forth a resolution urging the churches of the Southern Baptist Convention to raise $10,000. The purpose of this fund was to "aid young colored ministers in acquiring education and more perfect training for their work." At this juncture, I paused, allowing this resolution to settle in the minds of Liberty Hill parishioners. This resolution illuminated aspects of the SBC that are often overlooked. Retelling the story necessitates presenting both the positive and negative aspects, the successes alongside the failures, and the highs with the lows. Both sides are intertwined, even if one side carries more weight. While the SBC exhibited elements of unity for the sake of the gospel, it was important to acknowledge that America still grappled with the aftermath of the Civil War, and the country's climate was far from calm.

Truth stands alone as a crucial element for healing, and in retelling the story of the Southern Baptist Convention, resolutions have played a significant role in providing a comprehensive view that includes both positive and negative aspects. This approach helps prevent four pitfalls: lumping, ignoring, grouping, and discouraging. By acknowledging the nuances of history, one can avoid oversimplification, neglect of crucial details, stereotyping, and the discouragement that might arise from an incomplete or biased narrative. Embracing the complexities of the story fosters a more nuanced understanding and contributes to a more constructive dialogue about the past and its implications.

Lumping, or the generalization of an entire group, is a pitfall that should be avoided. It is essential to recognize that the label "racist organization" does not apply to all Southern Baptists. As someone who serves as the pastor of two predominantly white Southern Baptist churches, a faculty member in a predominantly white seminary, and a ten-year member of the SBC, I can attest that lumping all Southern Baptists into the racist category is unjust. In the spirit of truth-telling that encompasses both positives and negatives, there have been both encouraging and discouraging moments as an African American in the SBC. However, the positive moments have far outweighed the challenging ones. This can be attributed to the power of relationships. The willingness to engage in meaningful relationships is crucial for racial reconciliation. While it does not guarantee a utopia, it does require staying in relationships long enough to break through barriers and discover authentic friendship. Though acknowledging that the SBC is not without instances of racism, it is essential to resist the application of a racist generalization to an entire organization.

Ignoring, the intentional dismissal of anything positive about an organization or group of people, is a dynamic phenomenon that hinges on the level of hurt experienced by an organization or group. An illustrative example is the Liberty Hill parishioner who refused to let me perform the eulogy at her funeral, citing my affiliation with the SBC. Her intentional dismissal of the positive interactions between Liberty Hill parishioners and members of the SBC revealed the depth of her pain. Though it may seem defiant, her opposition to associating with the SBC opened a much-needed honest dialogue. Pretending has no place in achieving true racial reconciliation. Racial cordiality that masks honesty only produces great actors and entertainers, and it fails to attain genuine unity when true feelings are withheld by one or both parties. Ignoring, in this context, is a tool to expose patterns and behaviors contrary to biblical principles, making it a hindrance to restoration and the development of the next steps necessary for reaching racial reconciliation. It is an essential aspect of the process that allows for an honest assessment and addresses the root causes of pain and division.

Grouping, as the intentional exclusive association with familiar people and groups, is a natural inclination, and there is no objection to associating with like-minded people, cultures, or affiliations. However, achieving racial reconciliation requires intentional engagement with the unfamiliar. Preventing grouping does not mean isolation from the familiar; instead, it involves combining the familiar and unfamiliar until a new sense of familiarity is established. Liberty Hill's association with the SBC did not occur merely transactionally but began relationally through personal friendships, local church cooperation, and regional gatherings. As Liberty Hill parishioners and members of the SBC collaborated in events, community ministry, missionary welcomes, conferences, and communal worship, the appeal of being part of a convention that is aligned with the Great Commission fostered a like-minded connection worth pursuing. Had Liberty Hill remained exclusively associated with the familiar, the impact of the kingdom of God would not have reached as far. Hosting hundreds of missionaries from seven states, extending evangelistic efforts to Cleveland and vicinity, conducting church planting conferences, outreach carnivals, prayer walks, neighborhood evangelism, local association meetings, holiday concerts, and multicultural experiences—all played distinct roles in reaching toward racial reconciliation. However, none of these events happened without intentional efforts to bring people of all races and cultures together for the glory of God and the edification of his people. The intentional breaking down of barriers and the fostering of inclusive spaces became essential components in the journey toward racial reconciliation.

While worship services, concerts, evangelistic outreach, community giveaways, and teaching sessions are impactful within similar cultures or groups, they become truly marvelous when done among a diverse population, showcasing a togetherness seldom highlighted for all to see and experience. Progressing toward racial reconciliation requires the ability of seeing before being. Churches should be intentional about engaging with other ethnicities in worship services and events, as it opens the door to fellowship and other opportunities for deeper engagement. I recall a church-wide painting event that transformed into a worship service and evolved into a multiethnic worship service, then into a community carnival, followed by evangelistic outreach, an associational conference, a mission trip, a community giveaway, associational meetings, and a host of other events. This series of engagements eventually led to Liberty Hill parishioners volunteering as ushers at the annual convention. Intentionality is crucial for racial reconciliation, and creating ways to engage diverse groups, even if it seems nonimpactful, has the potential to generate various opportunities for further fellowship and understanding.

Retelling the story can indeed have a lasting impact on the pathway toward racial reconciliation. By sharing both the positive and negative aspects of the story, biases are limited and decisions toward unity become possible. This chapter has described the expected skepticism and apprehension of Liberty Hill Baptist Church members who willingly participated despite growing concerns. The presentation, coupled with the expression of devastating experiences from the South, revealed that racial reconciliation is a journey rather than a destination. As the presentation on racial reconciliation in the SBC continued, more challenges and the unimaginable odds of building a future became apparent. The opening session retold the story of a painful past and challenged Liberty Hill parishioners not to be dismayed by the truth of history seldom mentioned. While slavery's evils impacted the lives of generations, there remained potential for restoration and reconciliation in the commonalities of humanity. However, the next chapter would cast doubt on the definition of humanity as acts were violently celebrated that grieved the heart of God. The journey toward racial reconciliation would continue to unfold with complexities and uncertainties, emphasizing the ongoing nature of the work ahead.

2

Can We Release the Hurt?

In the forthcoming chapter, we will delve into the challenging theme of letting go of hurt in the pursuit of racial reconciliation. This sensitive question prompts concerns about whether releasing the pain erases the past, gives perpetrators undeserved freedom, or merely leads to symbolic gestures amid the persisting struggles of discrimination and bigotry. Acknowledging these nuanced considerations is essential for any sincere attempt at racial reconciliation. Before exploring the process of releasing hurt, it is crucial to understand the root causes that make this release necessary. Racial reconciliation, fair or not, demands an individual cost that many individuals are hesitant to bear. As the second session of the presentation unfolded, Liberty Hill parishioners were prepared to confront a dark period in American history spanning from 1893 to 1912—an era marked by a haunting discussion within the SBC concerning lynchings.

After a brief interlude of worship and prayer, I took a moment to forewarn those in attendance about the graphic nature of my forthcoming PowerPoint presentation, which would include distressing images. By 1893, the US population had swelled to fifty million, and lynchings were becoming alarmingly prevalent in the Deep South.[1] Freed African Americans grappled with the agony of witnessing friends and family members hanged from trees, set ablaze, and subjected to torture and mob violence. Astonishingly, lynchings in that era did not evoke the jaw-dropping anxiety one would expect today; instead, they became festivities celebrated by families, with images of these brutal events turned into widely distributed postcards.[2] An article published on January 27, 1921, in the *Memphis Press* described the burning of a black prisoner, Henry Lowery, as an "outstanding lynching success."

As I scrolled through various lynching images, I noticed a sustained silence from Liberty Hill parishioners, with one person exiting the chapel. I thought it was a silent rage resting in the room, but I have come to acknowledge the silence as paying respects to souls lost during the horrific season of lynching. However, Tennessee was not the only state with lynching issues. According to the *Orlando Sentinel,* blacks were more likely to be lynched in Florida than in

---

[1] Mike Bianchi Commentary and Scott Maxwell Commentary, "Lynching: Florida's Brutal Distinction," Orlando *Sentinel,* March 7, 1993, https://www.orlandosentinel.com/1993/03/07/lynching-floridas-brutal-distinction/.

[2] Adrian Florido, "How Black Activists Used Lynching Souvenirs to Expose American Violence," NPR, February 8, 2022, https://www.npr.org/2022/02/08/1078977454/race-racism-lynching-postcards-ahmaud-arbery-george-floyd.

any other state, which had one of the highest per capita percentages of black lynching victims. In Arkansas, white businessmen saw the unionization of black sharecroppers as a threat to their prosperity and took matters into their own hands, lynching over two hundred black men.

Not only was this the climate in the South, but it was also the climate surrounding the SBC—a climate riddled with innocent bloodshed, war, riots, and lynchings. As lynchings escalated uncontrollably throughout Southern states, the typically vocal SBC hesitated in issuing a resolution addressing the escalating death toll. However, one man, Charles Hillyer, displayed courage by putting forth a resolution that would pose a challenge to the faith of the SBC and set a course toward racial unity.[3]

Photographers captured horrid photos of the victims, turning images into postcards that were then mailed to some white family and friends. Lynchings became spectacles for thousands of male, female, and child onlookers. An article in the June 26, 1919, *New Orleans States* newspaper ominously announced, "3,000 will burn negro. Ellisville Mob will lynch John Hartfield at 5 o'clock this afternoon. Governor Bilbo says he is powerless to stop it."

Lynchings deeply affected some members of the SBC, and the most extensive resolution addressing this issue came with the Hillyer Resolutions in Chattanooga, Tennessee (1906). The Hillyer Resolutions, originating from the Georgia Convention, expressed deep disdain and concern for the nation's direction amid the

---

[3] "Hillyer Resolutions," sbc.net, May 1, 1906, https://www.sbc.net/resource-library/resolutions/hillyer-resolutions/.

atrocities of lynching. The initial part of this resolution specifically emphasized "the right for every man, woman, boy, or girl to be safe as they come and go in their homes whether such homes be in a castle or cabin." Focusing on the defenseless individuals being forcibly taken from their homes and lynched by mobs, the Hillyer Resolutions brought attention to the lawlessness in the society.

As I continued presenting the PowerPoint presentation for this extensive resolution, a parishioner interrupted to inquire about Southern Baptist participation in these lynchings. Although I had not extensively researched that topic, I was aware of at least one pastor who shared with me an account of a member in his congregation who spoke approvingly about a lynching he attended, describing it in a casual, matter-of-fact manner. While there may be other pastors with similar experiences, this resolution reflected the belief that "lynching blunts the public conscience, undermines the foundations on which society stands, and if unchecked will bring on anarchy." This resolution also recognized the escalation of the appalling tragedies and crimes, acknowledging that they "seem to be growing worse and more numerous."

Hate crimes and lynchings became so prevalent in almost all parts of the South. The resolution reflected the outrage at this situation and called on Southern Baptists to move beyond "merely writing, teaching, and praying against the lynchers," insisting that they provide the helpless and innocent victims of crime with "adequate or sufficient protection." The resolution emphasized the need for condemnation against these horrific crimes with equal, if not greater, emphasis. The SBC, at least in print, responded to the injustices. This resolution may appear to be simple words on a page, but messengers of the

SBC began constructing messages of support for those victimized. The significance of the Hillyer Resolutions cannot be understated. As law officers aided in discrimination, abuse, kidnappings, and mob lynchings, where could those abused find support? With court rulings failing to provide equal justice under the law, a voice outside the marginalized needed to bring awareness and attention to injustices.

As I shared this truth with the parishioners of Liberty Hill, it struck a chord and underscored the efforts made by Southern Baptists to at least voice their support for the marginalized. The Hillyer Resolutions appealed to the spirit of Southern Baptist members, urging them to be guided by the Word of God and offering prayers for the "agitation of the system." While this resolution did not mandate direct action, its purpose was to instill a spiritual obligation to confront societal injustices, with the hope "that the discussion of this important subject may be taken up and continued by the different state conventions and district associations until combined public sentiment shall demand and obtain the needed and appropriate remedies." This resolution does not suggest that every member of the SBC shared a uniform concern about the violent acts in society. However, a significant number of Southern Baptist messengers were disturbed enough to pass a resolution on behalf of the SBC, providing a voice to those who were disturbed.

A set of new resolutions on "law and order" laid out a framework for tackling societal inequalities. **The Recommendation on Law and Order—Richmond, Virginia (1907)** stated that the president should appoint a committee of "three to arrange a mass meeting to consider what may best be done by Christian men and ministers to create a more wholesome public opinion to make the criminal laws more certain, prompt, and effective."[4] This crucial resolution played a significant role in drawing attention to the lynching issues that afflicted society. With the law lacking two essential elements crucial for order—respect and effectiveness—vigilantes could impose their own form of justice, leading to random lynchings throughout Southern states.

Without the support of the law, individuals were indiscriminately seized from their homes and subjected to the will of their oppressors, perpetuating evil throughout society as crimes went unpunished. The SBC, in its early stages, began shedding light on these injustices stemming from a lopsided legal system. Liberty Hill parishioners observed how messengers from the SBC lent their voices to the societal atrocities. I am not asserting that the SBC saved lives, provided jobs, or facilitated opportunities for reconciliation; but a voice, however faint in the wilderness, cried out for Southern Baptists to take a stand against the blatant injustices in society. Again, the intent behind making this connection is not to absolve the SBC but to present researched documentation from the messengers of the SBC that merits inclusion in the narrative.

As messengers from the SBC found their societal voice against the atrocities in their communities, a natural progression occurred that extended to the marginalized. A six-year gap transpired following the 1907 resolution. After this gap, a significant resolution unfolded, revealing a noteworthy step for the SBC. As the SBC

---

[4] "Recommendation on Law and Order," sbc.net, May 1, 1907, https://www.sbc.net/resource-library/resolutions/recommendation-on-law-and-order/.

pursued justice for all, the National Convention of Colored Baptists developed a relationship that opened the door for dialogue, discussion, and opportunities to dream. Although there is no documentation of what led up to this subsequent resolution, there is enough indirect evidence to understand that as the National Convention of Colored Baptists extended its hand, the SBC reciprocated, and an agreement was formed.

While there was training and teaching for African Americans within the SBC, the **Resolution on Cooperation with Other Baptists—St. Louis, Missouri (1913)** marked the first major partnership of its kind.[5] The significance of this partnership presented, at the very least, a consideration of racial reconciliation. The National Convention of Colored Baptists, aiming to establish a theological seminary for the education of African American Baptist preachers, reached out to the SBC to seek advice and cooperation.

Liberty Hill parishioners asserted that this partnership existed because the National Convention of Colored Baptists did not attempt to join the SBC but sought to create their own institutions. While I acknowledged the insinuation, the convention's resolution to appoint a committee of nine "to advise and confer with the colored brethren on the subject" and pledge practical financial assistance as deemed appropriate "at a later date" meant an investment. I reminded the Liberty Hill parishioners that this resolution had to be brought to a vote by the messengers of the convention, and

[5] "Resolution on Cooperation with Other Baptists," sbc.net, May 1, 1913, https://www.sbc.net/resource-library/resolutions/resolution-on-cooperation-with-other-baptists-13/.

though we do not know the heart of both parties of the conversation, it passed and became an official resolution.

The SBC, often willing to provide resources, took small steps. Following the Civil War, political and legal powers clashed with the people's determination to ensure fair treatment and equal justice for all. The partnership between the National Convention of Colored Baptists and the SBC was a step in the right direction toward mending deep-seated hurt. At a time when America grappled with continued hostility toward people of color, this union offered a ray of hope amid the nation's struggle for stability.

The Civil Rights Act of 1866 emerged as the first federal law affirming equal protection under the law for all citizens, regardless of race or color.[6] With this act, justice reached millions of citizens who had been previously marginalized by their own nation. Opposed to the changing political and legal landscape, a segment of the population resisted, feeling their hold on power slipping away. In 1866, the Ku Klux Klan emerged in response to perceived political and social shifts. Employing tactics such as voter intimidation and targeted violence, they sought to eliminate perceived national threats. Despite these efforts, the Fourteenth and Fifteenth Amendments were ratified, and the Civil Rights Act of 1875 extended the sphere of civility for minorities.

---

[6] "Civil Rights Act of 1866, 'An Act to Protect All Persons in the United States in Their Civil Rights, and Furnish thc Means of Their Vindication,'" National Constitution Center.org, https://constitutioncenter.org/the-constitution/historic-document-library/detail/civil-rights-act-of-1866-april-9-1866-an-act-to-protect-all-persons-in-the-united-states-in-their-civil-rights-and-furnish-the-means-of-their-vindication.

Despite the hopeful tone I conveyed when discussing the collaboration between the National Convention of Colored Baptists and the SBC, members of Liberty Hill maintained a stoic air of indifference during this segment of the presentation. I remember a conversation about the ability of the National Convention of Colored Baptists to create opportunities independently of the SBC, and while the discussion had validity, the context was crucial. The partnership between the National Convention of Colored Baptists and the SBC took place in 1913, just fifty years after the devastating Civil War and the abolition of slavery.

In many Southern cities, white communities heavily relied on the SBC, which, over the years, had developed the Cooperative Program (a giving strategy for Southern Baptist churches to support missions and ministry), foreign mission boards, and various associational partnerships. African Americans, however, faced the legacies of slavery, discrimination, lynchings, and numerous obstacles to survival. Seeking support from the SBC was not only financially advantageous but also provided a certain level of protection and endorsement from a well-established institution in the South. The willingness of the National Convention of Colored Baptists to collaborate with the SBC reflected society's social progress and the Southern Baptists' readiness to participate in the growth and development of a colored convention.

At a time when lynchings were escalating, this engagement by the SBC demonstrated a commitment to ongoing training, funding, and outreach efforts, including financial support and access to other Southern Baptist resources. Releasing the hurt cannot occur in isolation because the perpetrated hurt did not happen in isolation. Racial reconciliation can only take shape in the presence of the "other." The partnership between the National Convention of Colored Baptists and the SBC, though not originally intended to have reconciliatory ramifications, created the potential for barrier-breaking experiences that continue to foster racial reconciliation.

In 1845, when the SBC prioritized educating the colored population, that gesture watered the seeds of racial reconciliation. In 1849, when the SBC urged pastors to inform their colored population of the opportunities for African missions, whether intentionally or not, the gesture watered the seed of racial reconciliation. In 1884, when the SBC saw the need for the instruction of colored preachers and deacons, the consequent resolution watered the seed of racial reconciliation. In 1886, when the SBC requested that $10,000 be raised to provide education and extensive training for colored ministers, they were watering the seed of racial reconciliation. In 1906, when the Hillyer Resolutions appealed for the Southern Baptist messengers to speak out and act against lynchings, they were watering the seed of racial reconciliation. In 1907, when the **Recommendation on Law and Order** critically examined the misuse of power that plagued society, seeds of racial reconciliation were watered.

In chapter 1, "Can We Retell the Story?" the truth remained essential. In chapter 2, "Can We Release the Hurt?" trust remains essential. However, establishing trust takes time. Trust, a significant five-letter word, can make people hesitant and inauthentic. Achieving trust can take years, but losing it can take seconds. Nevertheless, striving for racial reconciliation requires a level of trust that many people avoid. After all, history exposes stories of abuse, mistreatment, and alienation due to the one-sidedness of trust. How can racial reconciliation be reached if each party questions the trustworthiness of the other? Engaging with this reality makes racial reconciliation seem distant. However, racial unity remains costly and requires a willingness to seek trust in achieving steps toward racial reconciliation.

Living in New Orleans, Louisiana, I have learned that there is nothing like good food to unite people. Religious affiliation, political leanings, social status, or financial circumstance matters not when a good meal is on the table. So, what better way to connect with "others" than by breaking bread together? A simple invitation could be the difference between strangers and lasting friendships. Food crosses racial, ethnic, and international barriers. In 1999, I began my professional basketball career in Augsburg, Germany. As this was my first experience living overseas, my expectations were low. Disturbing images of concentration camps and human atrocities tainted my view of a nation formed twenty-six years after the founding of the SBC.

Upon arrival, I received an invitation to dine at the home of the team owner. I was unfamiliar with German cuisine but looked forward to the experience. After I rang his doorbell, the kids answered, gave a quick high five, and rushed past to play with pinecones and leaves, or so I thought. Afterward, they rushed back into the house and made a mess on the dining room table. With dirt fragments, pinecones, and leaves piled on the table, I knew their mother's displeasure would end in rage. She informed her children, in a broken English dialect, to "wash their hands for dinner." The language seemed harsh and short, but hey, I was no longer in America. Then she did something I did not expect. First, she did not kill her kids for throwing leaves, pinecones, and dirt fragments on the dining room table. Second, and most impressively, she took those leaves, pinecones, and dirt fragments; spread them across the dining room table; grabbed six candles from the pantry; and positioned them in various spots around the leaves, pinecones, and dirt fragments. Eating dinner with the smell of leaves and pinecones felt outdoorsy and natural. I learned much about the importance of a memorable dining experience that day, which stirred great conversation and helped me bond with the German family I had just met.

Food can be used as a secret weapon of racial reconciliation to break barriers and unite people. While food does not guarantee theological agreement, social justice alignment, or mutual interests, it offers an opportunity for dialogue that increases understanding, engages stereotypes, and provides meaningful time to consider racial reconciliation. While this seems like a no-brainer, many people need help taking the initial step to begin the simple process of eating together due to the intimate nature of the act. Try not to overthink it. Keep everything as simple as possible. Simply invite someone of a different ethnicity to a meal and let God do the rest. If they say, "No thank you," stay diligent and do not give up until a meal is complete.

Liberty Hill Baptist Church boasts a dining hall accommodating over two hundred people. Hosting the annual local associational meeting brought together multiple ethnicities for fellowship, worship, and yearly updates. Churches representing African Americans, Ukrainians, Anglo-Americans, Messianic Jews, Hispanics, Bhutanese, Egyptians, and deaf communities presented annual updates and highlights. With a representation of over thirty churches, songs, sermonettes, liturgical dances, and deaf presentations, the annual associational meeting stood multifaceted, displaying evidence of God's grace.

While seemingly insignificant, food can aid in the process of releasing the hurt and reveal a pathway for healing. Releasing the hurt is not "getting over it" but engaging with "it" for a deeper understanding and method for moving forward. "Getting over it" does not deal with the hurt but ignores it and does not provide the growth necessary for the pathway toward racial reconciliation. "Getting over it" stunts the growth of self, limits the growth of others, and covers the steps of racial reconciliation needed for unity. Any meaningful engagement is helpful for racial reconciliation, and food can provide the opportunity.

In 2015, Columbus, Ohio, hosted the SBC. The host state provided ushers during the annual meeting proceedings, and Liberty Hill members volunteered. Although Liberty Hill members had never attended the SBC before, the opportunity to participate and attend meant engaging with Southern Baptist national messengers. Liberty Hill members not only served but also stayed to experience the events of the convention firsthand. This included interacting with missionaries commissioned abroad, listening to church planters share updates and testimonies, participating in multiple worship services, and witnessing the process of how resolutions are presented and voted on—an experience that cannot be simulated in any other way. These interactions contributed to moving the needle toward racial reconciliation and set the stage for chapter 3, focusing on reestablishing trust.

3

Can We Reestablish the Trust?

In the last two chapters, the themes of truth and trust played crucial roles in the progress of racial reconciliation. Chapter 1, titled "Can We Retell the Story?" unveiled the previously unknown narrative of the SBC, enabling Liberty Hill parishioners to form their own conclusions. Chapter 2, "Can We Release the Hurt?" underscored the significance of relationships and community as a healing force. It emphasized that overcoming cultural isolation requires intentional efforts to connect and advance racial reconciliation, creating space for healing and understanding. This chapter focuses on reestablishing connections and showcases Southern Baptists' desire to address the needs of the marginalized.

After the 1913 partnership with the National Convention of Colored Baptists, thirty years transpired before another resolution surfaced addressing the concerns of African Americans. When presenting this section to the members of Liberty Hill Baptist Church, I emphasized that the absence of resolutions does not necessarily indicate a lack of engagement by Southern Baptist messengers. Instead, I pointed out that American priorities, including church finance, religious liberties, peace, student loans, prohibition, drugs, evangelism, missions, persecution in Romania, beauty contests, politics, and the Social Service Commission, took precedence and diverted attention from issues impacting African Americans. Additionally, international conflicts like Pearl Harbor, the atomic bomb, Hitler, and the World Wars shifted America's priorities.

Liberty Hill parishioners warmly remembered Thomas Austin, a member who served as part of the Tuskegee Airmen. After attending the Tuskegee Institute in Alabama in 1941, Austin broke racial barriers to achieve the rank of staff sergeant and aircraft mechanic during World War II. It was my honor and privilege to serve as Austin's pastor. Our shared experiences included celebrating the 2012 motion picture *Red Tails*, which brought a smile to his face as he reminisced about the various interviews and red-carpet events he attended with family and friends. Our time together involved stories of his service in the all-black squadron and his crucial responsibilities in keeping the planes in the air. The pressure not to fail drove Austin to greatness, and he felt pride upon learning that the Tuskegee Airmen received credit for shooting down or damaging 400 enemy aircrafts. On January 25, 2014, I had the honor of delivering the eulogy for this war hero at Liberty Hill Baptist Church. Austin's indelible contribution to America is forever recorded in the annals of American history, and his love for people of all races continues to inspire my commitment to racial reconciliation.

While the Great Depression, rumors of wars, and the looming threat of atomic bombs captured the attention of Southern Baptists, ministry issues that were once neglected began to surface. State conventions, local associations, and mission efforts made the annual SBC meetings crucial for exchanging information, addressing concerns, and devising strategies. However, as SBC messengers attended to national affairs and the needs of churches and pastors, lynchings, primarily targeting African Americans, remained a concerning issue.

In 1936, thirty years after the initial Hillyer Resolutions, Southern Baptist messengers passed the **Resolution on Lynching and Mob Violence—St. Louis, Missouri (1936).**[1] As I continued the presentation for Liberty Hill Baptist Church parishioners, the stark reality that mob violence persisted in society hit closer to home. Liberty Hill parishioners shared stories of the challenges of living in the South, where violence, lack of job opportunities, and the desire for a better life for the next generation led them to join the Great Migration, which included six million African Americans leaving the South for improved opportunities. This resolution urged white pastors to preach "from time to time upon the sanctity of human life under an orderly government" to create and maintain law and order. It called on SBC members to demand that officers faithfully perform their duty to protect the rights of all accused or condemned persons in their charge. The resolution

[1] "Resolution on Lynching and Mob Violence," sbc.net, May 1, 1936, https://www.sbc.net/resource-library/resolutions/resolution-on-lynching-on-mob-violence/.

concluded with an expression of dissatisfaction until "lynchings shall cease and mob violence shall be completely banished."

Through this resolution, SBC messengers urged pastors to use pulpits and teachers to use Sunday school, Bible study sessions, prayer meetings, and letters to Congress to combat lynchings. The partnership and open-door policy formed with the National Convention of Colored Baptists created the kind of dialogue needed to establish lines of communication and support. This resolution, coupled with actions by the members of the SBC, would begin to turn the tide on lynchings. The number of lynchings began to decrease and would be acknowledged in future resolutions.

The attention that the SBC gave to lynchings and mob violence in their resolutions demonstrated the convention's influence in the South. Acknowledging the resolutions associated with each appeal filled the knowledge gap for Liberty Hill parishioners. The records showed, at least in print, that the horrific crimes against many African Americans did not go unnoticed by the SBC. However, with the appeal for Southern Baptists to write Congress, preach, teach, and prioritize the decrease of lynchings, a seldom-mentioned aspect of communication is often overlooked: the social justice tenet of the SBC.

Reaching the masses meant communicating through the church, as preachers and teachers were heralds for the Lord and in society. While typically associated with African American churches, the SBC compelled pastors and spiritual leaders to use pulpits and other means to disseminate messages to its members through the churches for influencing society. Evidently, the strategy worked because the subsequent resolution on lynchings claimed a minor victory.

In 1939, the **Resolution Concerning Lynching and Race Relations—Oklahoma City, Oklahoma (1939)** highlighted the continuation of lynchings but expressed gratitude that the numbers had significantly decreased.[2] The SBC cited public pressures to halt mass mob attacks, the demand for law enforcement to responsibly execute their jobs, and the demand for the legal system to crack down on vigilantes as reasons for gratitude. For in the year 1938, "the number of lynchings decreased and only six lives were sacrificed to mob violence." Although six too many, the resolution continued with "a deep sense of sorrow and shame to us, both as citizens and Christians, that this form of lawlessness should persist to any degree and that we pledge ourselves and urge all citizens to contend earnestly for the administration of justice under the orderly processes of law, reaffirming our unalterable opposition to all forms of mob violence."

The SBC also acknowledged that racial animosities were growing less and racial understanding and cooperation were increasing, "as indicated by the fact that the white people of the South, especially our Baptist pastors and churches, are establishing and maintaining frequent contacts of a friendly and helpful nature with the Negro race." The SBC urged friendly and helpful contacts and relations, remembering that "the strong should bear the burdens of the weak."

---

[2] "Resolution Concerning Lynching and Race Relations," sbc.net, May 1, 1939, https://www.sbc.net/resource-library/resolutions/resolution-concerning-lynching-and-race-relations/.

The SBC also recognized disparities among the races and used this resolution to begin addressing "the many inequalities and injustices which still exist in the dealings of organized society and of individuals with the Negro race and in the provision made for the advancement of the Negro race, such as the disproportionate distribution of public school funds, the lack of equal and impartial administration of justice in the courts. . . ." This resolution encouraged the members of the convention to correct inequalities by providing opportunities for supporting those in need.

In print, the SBC took significant steps toward racial reconciliation. Despite the challenge some Liberty Hill parishioners faced in embracing the language, a deeper understanding and appreciation of the information emerged. For those at Liberty Hill who endured societal prejudices, discussing slavery, lynchings, and other atrocities triggered an emotional pain. As the Liberty Hill parishioners carefully considered the words, I encouraged the practice of grace, particularly when hosting visiting missionaries. As cultures rebuild trust through various interactions, a collective embrace of a culture of grace becomes crucial. In a society prone to dismissiveness and "cancel culture," a single honest mistake could jeopardize a reputation, a relationship, or even a career. However, extending grace can allow for a sustained dialogue that reveals true intentions. This, in turn, can deepen the commitment to racial reconciliation and promote constructive conversations. The significance of grace becomes richer as time for meaningful dialogue nurtures promising relationships. Racial reconciliation is a gradual process, and any interruption in the journey delays efforts, potentially causing pauses and restarts. Joining the SBC offered Liberty Hill members numerous opportunities to forge new relationships within the broader Southern Baptist community.

Hosting conferences and meetings at Liberty Hill Baptist Church brought together missionaries from across the nation, spanning from Texas to Florida, Georgia to North Carolina. These individuals traveled from diverse places with the common purpose of spreading the gospel, participating in regional conferences, and supporting church planters. As the host pastor, I had the opportunity to engage with each group and to explore different cultures with every new visitor. Every ministry had its unique focus, and spending time with these groups involved answering questions about the city, discussing the impact of ministry, and recommending good places to eat. Although I cherished interactions with all the groups, a particularly impactful moment occurred when a group of young adults engaged me in a weighty discussion following an evangelistic outreach. The emotional tone of the conversation caught me off guard, but I recognized that if I was advocating for parishioners to extend grace, I needed to do the same. After receiving an evangelistic report, two students approached me with heartfelt apologies for their previous mentality toward Liberty Hill Baptist Church and the city of Cleveland. At that moment, their apology took me by surprise; they expressed regret for having believed they were superior to individuals of African descent. Initially, I questioned whether I had heard them correctly, but the sincerity reflected in everyone's expressions and the tears in their eyes made it clear that this was not going to be a typical conversation. For the first time in my five years as a member of the SBC, I found myself engaged in an honest and open conversation.

Extending grace in the context of racial reconciliation involves listening and responding without negative emotional attachments. Progress in advancing racial understanding often requires navigating through the maze of unaware insensitivities, where moments and actions can strain relations among cultures. In this journey, both tension and grace play crucial roles in laying the foundation for reconciliation. Tension, though potentially detrimental, when it is coupled with grace, strikes the right balance for growth and understanding.

I recall an incident when setting up my classroom for a lecture series. Several students walked in, glanced at me, and left the room to check the marquee. After this repeated a few times, I invited them to sit down, explaining that I was the lecturer for the day. Similarly, with the young missionaries at Liberty Hill, we sat down for forty-five minutes, engaging in a hopeful conversation about breaking stereotypes and myths, working together toward a more inclusive future. Avoiding sensitivity and extending grace became paramount. Drawing from my experiences with more profound levels of discrimination, I believe these moments can serve as opportunities to reestablish trust and build a more profound connectivity that extends beyond cultural fellowships in hopes of meaningful relationships.

As I continued my presentation for Liberty Hill parishioners, the Southern Baptist messengers engaged in a significant discussion on race, culminating in the passage of the **Resolution Concerning Race Relations—Baltimore, Maryland (1940)**. Within this resolution, convention messengers "expressed satisfaction that mob killings had nearly ceased."[3] While acknowledging the ongoing work required, they celebrated the growing cooperation between African Americans and members of the SBC. The resolution pledged a commitment to ensure that African Americans receive "equal and impartial justice before the courts, better and more equitable opportunities in the industry, and a more equitable share in public funds and education." Although this proactive resolution did not eliminate racial inequalities, it demonstrated a willingness among the messengers of the SBC to advocate against injustices. During the 1940 SBC meeting, messengers continued to address a spectrum of issues from the local, state, and national levels. Their voices provided a platform for the voiceless, challenging national leaders on various fronts. Southern Baptists opposed the US president's choice of ambassador to the Vatican, spoke against churches becoming recruiting stations for war efforts, challenged the freedom of the press regarding unwholesome literature in local newspaper stands, expressed grief over the lives lost annually due to alcohol, contested aspects of the social security act, voted to broadcast sermons from selected ministers on public radio, and collected funds for the American Bible Society. Each convention raised issues that addressed the nation's moral compass while simultaneously advancing the gospel message. As questions poured in from Liberty Hill parishioners regarding how Southern Baptist resolutions supported

[3] "Resolution Concerning Race Relations," sbc.net. May 1, 1940, https://www.sbc.net/resource-library/resolutions/resolution-concerning-race-relations/

the concerns of African Americans, the harsh realities of the civil rights movement added a layer of complexity.

During this time, resolutions seemingly advocated for the advancement of African Americans. With messengers urging local, state, and national leaders to establish, uphold, and enforce laws for the equality of all people, the SBC appeared to be positioned for great steps toward racial reconciliation. As my presentation delved deeper into the historical resolutions of the SBC, many Liberty Hill parishioners found themselves unaware of the convention messengers' expressions of displeasure regarding the mistreatment, lynching, and suffering of African Americans in the "land of the free." Reading resolutions advocating for the advancement of African Americans left some parishioners questioning the authenticity of the presented information. However, I reassured them that the information was well documented and could be easily verified online or by visiting the Southern Baptist Historical Library and Archives in Nashville, Tennessee.

The Resolution Concerning Race Relations—Birmingham, Alabama (1941) further underscored the SBC messengers' commitment to dismantling racial inequalities.[4] This resolution not only reaffirmed the "welfare of all races" but also explicitly committed to the "interest and advancement" of African Americans. With the total African American population at ten million, Southern Baptist messengers appealed to pastors and church leaders to foster

[4] "Resolution Concerning Race Relations," sbc.net, May 1, 1941, https://www.sbc.net/resource-library/resolutions/resolution-concerning-race-relations-2/.

"the finest Christian spirit and attitude toward the Negro race" and to actively contribute to the welfare of the race, both economically and religiously, while defending and protecting all civil rights. Despite the seemingly unifying language of the resolution, some parishioners at Liberty Hill responded with dismissive gestures. I recognized the difficulty for Liberty Hill parishioners to reconcile the unifying language with the detrimental historical actions of the past. The presentation was pushing against their guarded perspectives; it was contrary to their life stories and personal experiences.

The Resolution on Ministerial Education for Negro Baptists—Atlanta, Georgia (1944) marked another significant point in the SBC's commitment to racial progress.[5] It highlighted the continuation of the convention's partnership with the National Convention of Colored Baptists, as established in the **Resolution on Cooperation with Other Baptists—St. Louis, Missouri (1913)**.[6] This connection was not merely symbolic; the actions that followed demonstrated the SBC's dedication to their words. The tangible outcome of this commitment emerged in the form of the American Baptist Theological Seminary in Nashville, Tennessee. This institution became a testament to the SBC's efforts to provide continual education and training for African American Baptist preachers. However, the reactions from Liberty Hill parishioners

---

[5] "Resolution On Ministerial Education For Negro Baptists," sbc.net May 1, 1944, https://www.sbc.net/resource-library/resolutions/resolution-on-ministerial-education-for-negro-baptists/

[6] "Resolution On Cooperation With Other Baptists," sbc.net, May 1, 1913, https://www.sbc.net/resource-library/resolutions/resolution-on-cooperation-with-other-baptists-13/

persisted with some sighs and groans. The complexity of these historical truths contrasted with individual experiences. While the SBC, as an institution, demonstrated support, not every member eagerly embraced the advancement of African Americans.

Reflecting on the conversations with Liberty Hill parishioners following this segment of the presentation, I experienced mixed emotions. On one side, I actively engaged in various roles within the SBC—serving as a pastor and a doctoral student and participating in a range of activities such as organizing events, hosting missionaries, teaching courses, leading worship, and contributing to our local executive boards. On the other side, I remained deeply connected to a black community that played a significant role in my life. This community raised, trained, encouraged, supported, and believed in me through various life stages. The community was there for me during college, taught me the Bible in Sunday school and vacation Bible school, provided encouragement when others doubted, celebrated my successes, championed me in times of need, empathized with my struggles, and inspired me to pursue my God-given potential. However, even within this supportive community, I acknowledged the existence of factions unwilling to pursue racial reconciliation. Despite the challenges in both communities, the common foundation of Christianity offered a potential bridge for racial reconciliation. The shared commitment to Christian principles and values should be the unifying force, offering hope for overcoming difficulties that accompany the pursuit of racial harmony.

The Resolution on Race—Miami, Florida (1946) laid bare the existence of factions within the SBC that stood opposed to the progress toward racial equality.[7] While church autonomy, a key principle of the SBC, allows individual churches the freedom to decide how to respond to resolutions, it also introduces the potential for internal conflict within the convention. Despite the written show of support for African American progress, this resolution revealed an undermining faction attempting to hinder the strides made in supporting the marginalized. The danger of autonomy became evident in the face of this internal conflict, threatening to undermine years of progress and unity within the SBC. **The Resolution on Race** addressed this conflict head-on, acknowledging "the efforts of groups" within the convention that sought to "breed hate and confusion." As I highlighted this resolution, Liberty Hill parishioners gained insight into the internal challenges faced by the SBC. The resolution emphasized the importance of maintaining integrity by revealing and addressing internal conflicts. It called upon the spirit of Southern Baptist churches, declaring the significance of faith and that the "teachings of the Lord expressly forbid hatred." Moreover, it urged members of Southern Baptist churches to "refrain from associating with groups that aimed to foment strife and division based on differences of race," religion, and culture. By acknowledging these internal challenges, the SBC demonstrated a commitment to taking responsibility and discouraging enmity within its ranks. The resolution served as a call to action in the pursuit of unity, emphasizing the shared values of faith and the rejection of hatred.

---

[7] "Resolution on Race," sbc.net, May 1, 1946, https://www.sbc.net/resource-library/resolutions/resolution-on-race-3/.

By addressing members and churches that undermined the optimism toward racial reconciliation, the SBC not only challenged them but also urged a shift toward a biblical worldview instead of an earthly perspective. The resolution went beyond rhetoric and included actionable steps. A diverse committee of nine people was appointed, comprising representatives from the Home Mission Board, the American Baptist Theological Seminary, the Committee on Negro Theological Education, the Public Relations Committee, the Social Service Commission, and four additional members. Their mandate was to thoroughly review the services provided by Southern Baptists to the Negro race. This resolution demonstrated the SBC's commitment to addressing internal challenges and fostering racial reconciliation. By appealing to Christian virtues and divine authority, the messengers aligned with the biblical mandate of loving one another. In doing so, they countered the prevailing societal emphasis on self-interest with a call to prioritize unity and understanding, reflecting the principles of a biblical worldview.

The Social Service Committee Recommendation Concerning Race Relations—Chicago, Illinois (1950) represented a resolution that applauded the Home Mission Board's leadership for inviting African American churches to participate in simultaneous revival plans.[8] The resolution expressed the belief that "if plans continued and expanded in the following years through local and associational planning committees, it would significantly advance

---

[8] "Social Service Committee Recommendation Concerning Race Relations," sbc.net, May 1, 1950, https://www.sbc.net/resource-library/resolutions/social-service-committee-recommendation-concerning-race-relations-adopted/.

Christian cooperation in race relations."This resolution underscored the ongoing efforts of the SBC to maintain connections with the African American community, primarily through the shared worship of God. Despite existing tension within the SBC, there was a steadfast commitment to remain grounded in biblical principles as foundational to the work of religious communities. The resolution reflected a determination to stay connected to the African American community, guided by a faith-driven approach. In the face of societal challenges and internal tensions, faith emerged as the driving force for unity. The emphasis on faith became a powerful counterbalance, gradually reducing the impact of worldly noise, and this shift toward faith as a guiding principle reinforced the SBC's commitment to fostering connections and cooperation with the African American community and demonstrated that the determining factor went beyond societal reach and understanding. Faith became the unifying and transformative force that fueled the pursuit of unity and understanding amid complexity.

4

Can We Reduce the Noise?

External noise is a significant obstacle in the pursuit of racial reconciliation. How can one navigate and filter through the sounds? On May 25, 2020, the tragic killing of George Floyd reverberated globally, eliciting widespread calls for justice.[1] The universally witnessed nine-minute and twenty-nine-second video led to the conviction of Derek Chauvin, a white Minneapolis police officer, who pressed his knee onto Floyd's neck as he lay handcuffed on the street. On March 12, 2021, the Minneapolis City Council approved a settlement of $27 million for George Floyd's family.[2] Despite this, Floyd's death ignited protests

---

[1] Jason Silverstein, "The Global Impact of George Floyd: How Black Lives Matter Protests Shaped Movements around the World," *CBS News*, last modified June 4, 2021, https://www.cbsnews. com/news /george-floyd-black-lives-matter-impact/.

[2] Amy Forliti, "Prosecutors: Officer Was on Floyd's Neck for about 9 Minutes," *AP News*, last modified March 4, 2021, https://apnews.com

worldwide, with people of various ages, races, and ethnicities expressing their collective outrage. While the concerns of other races and ethnicities were well intentioned, they weighed heavily on many African Americans, sparking questions about what it means to be "black in America." The ensuing discussions found platforms in made-for-TV specials, podcasts, social media channels, college lecture halls, and even church pulpits, turning into crucial destinations for learning about African American struggles with law enforcement.

Numerous hours were spent engaging in conversations with white colleagues, friends, and neighbors who sought to grasp the black experience in America. Like many African Americans during this period of heightened awareness, I patiently fielded questions and addressed concerns from white colleagues who struggled to comprehend the daily profiling, stares, antagonistic remarks, and subtle gestures that I, along with countless other African Americans, endure regularly.

After an extensive conversation with a white colleague, I chose to relate an encounter I had with law enforcement while returning home from a Florida memorial service for a family member of one of my parishioners. That night, I observed red and blue lights in the rearview mirror, a scenario all too familiar. Despite the familiarity, I remained composed and followed a personal protocol. First, I rolled down all the windows in my vehicle. Second, I turned on all the interior lights of the vehicle. Third, I kept my hands on the

---

/article/trials-derek-chauvin-minneapolis-racial-injustice-060f6e9e8b7079505a1b096a68311c2b.

steering wheel. Fourth, I did not move. Fifth, I allowed the officer to initiate the conversation. Finally, I included my college identification when asked for my driver's license. While these six steps may appear extreme and perhaps unnecessary, most black males have their own modified versions of steps they follow when stopped by the police. Regardless of the specific steps, the shared goal among all black men is simple: to return home safely.

Let me elaborate on the rationale behind each step. First, I rolled down the windows of my vehicle to dispel any potential imagination the approaching officers might have. I wanted to convey transparency, assuring them that I had nothing to hide. Second, I turned on the interior lights to further eliminate misunderstandings and reinforce the openness communicated in the first step. Third, I kept my hands on the steering wheel and in clear sight to ensure visibility to officers on both sides of my vehicle. Fourth, I refrained from making sudden movements, except for turning my head to look directly into the officers' eyes with every spoken word. This was a deliberate effort to establish a clear and respectful communication channel. Fifth, I allowed the officer to initiate the conversation, recognizing that, at that moment, my words might not carry as much weight as my cooperative demeanor. Finally, I included my college identification along with my driver's license and registration to communicate responsibility. While these steps may seem excessive, each one has the potential to eliminate a question, reduce pull over time, or secure civil treatment. The ensuing conversation involved the officer asking about my whereabouts at that late hour. First of all, it was just after 9:00 p.m. Second, as a husband of twenty-eight years and a father of four kids, my responsibilities extended beyond a simple curfew. Faced with this situation, I had two choices: assert my right to know why I was pulled over or respond to the officer's question. But being outnumbered in the dark in the middle of nowhere and pulled over on a roadside in Florida meant responding to every question with confidence and clarity.

I refer to the officer's initial question as "the articulation test." In my opinion, and based on my experiences, the officer was not necessarily concerned about my destination or purpose; rather, it was a quick interrogation to assess my articulation and gather preliminary information about the person pulled over. Understanding that I would not get a second chance to make a good first impression, I knew the importance of responding effectively. At that moment, my primary goal was to articulate my situation clearly. I explained that I was the pastor of a church in New Orleans and that I had members who had experienced a death in their family. I emphasized my intention to be there to support them. Furthermore, I proactively presented my identification to the officers before knowing why I was pulled over. At that juncture, the reason for the stop was secondary; all that mattered was that my wife needed a husband, and my kids needed a father.

After I presented my identification, the officer stated, "I pulled you over because you were weaving." A shock reverberated through my mind, evident in the subtle folding of my lips. Maintaining as much respect as possible, I responded with a composed, "Yes, sir." Throughout the night, I fielded multiple questions about my profession, livelihood, residence, and travel time. Each inquiry was met with a calm and steady voice. Upon verifying my license and registration, the officer remarked, "You seem like a good guy; I'll let you go."

I expressed gratitude, and six and a half hours later, I safely arrived home. Yet these rides home are always characterized by silence and reflection. While I acknowledge that not all officers would have treated me the same way, this experience and my established protocols for similar situations underscore the way people of color must navigate encounters amid discussions on the dangers of "driving while black" in social media, television, news outlets, and even conversations with close friends and family. When I recount this familiar experience to my white colleagues, they vehemently assert that the officer had no right to treat me in that manner, and I have to explain what it is like to be black in America. However, I am acutely aware that not all stories conclude with such positive outcomes.

On November 29, 2012, the killings of unarmed Timothy Russell and Malissa Williams sent shockwaves akin to the tragedy of George Floyd. The incident in Cleveland, Ohio, gripped the region as news spread of a twenty-three-minute car chase through the city, concluding with thirteen officers firing a total of 137 shots at a car that allegedly backfired while passing the Cleveland police headquarters. Officer Michael Brelo, positioned on the hood of the car, discharged 49 bullets directly into the windshield. This incident was later depicted in a Netflix series titled *137 Shots*.[3]

I personally attended the courthouse proceedings on the day the verdict was announced. Officer Michael Brelo was acquitted

---

[3] "'137 Shots' Documentary Explores Fatal Shooting of Timothy Russell and Malissa Williams Debuts Wed," *News 5 Cleveland WEWS*, last modified December 15, 2021, https://www.news5cleveland.com/news/137-shots/137-shots-documentary-explores-fatal-shooting-of-timothy-russell-and-malissa-williams-debuts-wed.

of all counts, and the city of Cleveland became the focal point of global attention. I found myself unexpectedly consoling the first cousin of the deceased victim, who stood directly in front of me. She fell into my arms, devastated by the verdict and the tragic loss of her family member. As I attempted to help her to her feet, news reporters from CNN, MSNBC, and various other outlets encircled us with cameras in our faces. When I woke up that morning, I had not anticipated that I would find myself in such a moment. What followed was a spontaneous protest outside the courthouse along Ontario Street, which organically evolved into a sizable march involving concerned citizens from the city. Despite the significant demands of the city, the march was a representation of diverse ethnicities, races, professions, faiths, generations, and social classes.

What had initially been perceived as a primarily black issue transformed into a cause that garnered support from individuals of every nationality and race. Images from the verdict were broadcast across the nation by news outlets and morning papers. Notably, the assembled crowd was not exclusively black; it was visibly diverse. Individuals from different backgrounds, including guys from the neighborhood, stood alongside schoolteachers, biker enthusiasts, dentists, doctors, skaters, and mothers. It was a striking demonstration of balanced support. Reducing the noise is about preventing the pains of society from deterring racial unity. Indeed, reducing the noise appears to be a formidable challenge in the face of numerous external events, conversations, news reports, podcasts, TikTok videos, and experiences.

As I prepared my researched presentation for the members of Liberty Hill, I took a moment to examine the anonymous survey feedback from forty-two parishioners. The survey was designed to evoke responses to specific statements intentionally crafted to challenge, provoke, unsettle, and potentially irritate the members of Liberty Hill. The objective was to assess the impact of external influences on their willingness to engage in racial reconciliation. I feared that the prevalent echoes of discrimination might impede their ability to actively pursue meaningful reconciliation. The survey included statements that touched on personal preferences, conventional knowledge, and faith leanings. Participants were instructed to indicate their level of agreement or disagreement on a scale with three subcategories: strongly, moderately, and slightly. It is important to highlight that the survey took place before the presentation, and the results are as follows:

> **Statement #1:** "Slavery impacts my relationship with Caucasians."
>
> **Average response:** Moderately agree.

The survey revealed that Liberty Hill parishioners acknowledged a moderate impact of slavery on their relationships with Caucasians. The historical context, with many parishioners having Southern roots and familial connections to individuals who lived through historical challenges, influenced their perspectives. Conversations with grandparents and great-grandparents, some with firsthand knowledge of these challenges, served as a reminder of the struggles faced by family members, neighbors, and friends. Despite the passage of time, the reduction of mental noise concerning this historical legacy remains a challenge for many Liberty Hill parishioners. Joining the SBC, an institution founded during the era of slavery, was seen as a complex decision that brought forth painful stories from the past.

> **Statement #2:** "Racial reconciliation is nice to pursue but will not be accomplished in my lifetime."
>
> **Average response:** Slightly disagree.

The survey indicated that, on average, parishioners at Liberty Hill leaned toward a slight disagreement with the notion that racial reconciliation is an idealistic pursuit unlikely to be achieved in their lifetime. However, the concept of racial reconciliation being perceived as merely "nice" was seen as potentially hindering progress. There was a suggestion that if the goal is solely to be nice, a deeper level of commitment may be sabotaged, impeding the collective work required to foster societal growth. Conversations with Liberty Hill parishioners unveiled a prevailing attitude of "Don't bother me, and I won't bother you" concerning racial reconciliation. This mentality, seen as a preferred version of reconciliation, was deemed to potentially undermine the joy of relationships and deprive the community of deeper and more meaningful experiences. Joining the SBC offered opportunities for parishioners to engage with members of the larger Baptist community. The hope was that, during worship services, a genuine spirit of unity would prevail, opening hearts to receive one another as brothers and sisters in Christ.

> **Statement #3:** "Faith overrides flesh regarding my racial tendencies."
>
> **Average response:** Moderately agree.

The survey reflected that, on average, Liberty Hill parishioners moderately agreed with the idea that faith should override flesh when it comes to racial tendencies. However, the presentation acknowledged that some parishioners, despite their strong foundation in the church and understanding of Christian virtues, faced challenges when faith was put to the test in the context of societal inclinations. The difficulties were particularly evident in discussions about joining the SBC, as some parishioners expressed a sense of historical loss. Recognizing this sentiment, I was encouraged to increase faith as a means of navigating and overcoming these challenges. The presentation aimed to bridge the gap between faith and the reality of societal influences, emphasizing the transformative power of faith in addressing racial tendencies.

> **Statement #4:** "If the Southern Baptist Convention changed its name, it would attract more African Americans."
>
> **Average response:** Moderately disagree.

The survey results showed that, on average, Liberty Hill parishioners moderately disagreed with the notion that a name change for the SBC would attract more African Americans. Discussions about the potential for a name change did not strongly resonate with the parishioners, likely influenced by the historical association with slavery. Many at Liberty Hill viewed a name change as a relatively inconsequential matter, emphasizing the importance of acknowledging and owning history.

> **Statement #5:** "White missionaries from the South have little to no impact doing ministry in urban areas."
>
> **Average response:** Moderately disagree.

The survey indicated that, on average, Liberty Hill parishioners moderately disagreed with the statement suggesting that white missionaries from the South have little or no impact when doing ministry in urban areas. Comments from parishioners highlighted the white savior complex and expressed a nuanced perspective on the effectiveness of ministry in urban areas. While there was no disagreement about the positive impact of sharing the gospel in urban communities, the notion of whites coming to save or help the poor blacks needed refinement. The presentation emphasized the importance of overcoming such barriers by promoting collaborative service in all communities and thereby fostering a deeper connection and understanding that contributes to racial reconciliation.

> **Statement #6:** "Workshops on racial reconciliation have little to no impact on racial reconciliation."
>
> **Average response:** Moderately disagree.

The survey results showed that, on average, Liberty Hill parishioners moderately disagreed with the statement suggesting that workshops on racial reconciliation have little or no impact on achieving reconciliation. Yet the challenges associated with such workshops were acknowledged, including repeated conversations from similar events and hearing the same old thing without changing. However, my presentation aimed to provide new knowledge about the SBC, offering information previously unknown to the parishioners of Liberty Hill Baptist Church.

> **Statement #7:** "It is hard to forgive former Ku Klux Klan members for acts against African Americans."
>
> **Average response:** Moderately agree.

The survey results indicated that, on average, Liberty Hill parishioners moderately agreed with the statement that forgiving former Ku Klux Klan members for acts against African Americans is challenging. Most responses fell between slight and moderate agreement, with few indicating slight disagreement. Notably, there were no responses of strong agreement. Some participants expressed a belief rooted in the idea of Jesus's example but admitted that they needed more time than the Savior to forgive. The complexity of forgiving individuals associated with the Ku Klux Klan was evident in the responses, emphasizing the ongoing struggle to reconcile forgiveness with historical acts of injustice.

> **Statement #8:** "The Southern Baptist Convention is a racist organization."
>
> **Average response:** Strongly disagree.

The survey results showed that, on average, Liberty Hill parishioners strongly disagreed with the statement suggesting that the SBC is a racist organization. Though they acknowledged concerns about the historical context of the SBC, none of the participants labeled the entire organization as racist. However, there was a recognition among parishioners that factions within the SBC might harbor elements of racism, and there were concerns about certain churches within the convention not being welcoming to African Americans in their fellowship. This nuanced perspective acknowledged the complexities within the organization while differentiating between the convention as a whole and specific factions or practices.

> **Statement #9:** "Christians have not been a shining example of racial reconciliation."
>
> **Average response:** Moderately agree.

The survey results indicated that, on average, Liberty Hill parishioners moderately agreed with the statement suggesting that

Christians have not been a shining example of racial reconciliation. This response highlighted a concern about the lack of love within Christian communities, preventing the world from witnessing the unity that Jesus's disciples are called to exhibit (John 13:35). The presentation aimed to address this concern by emphasizing the infectious nature of God's love and its potential to foster racial reconciliation within a community. The acknowledgment that there was room for improvement underscored the importance of actively working toward being a more compelling example of unity and love in the context of racial reconciliation.

> **Statement #10:** "Racism still exists but in different forms."
>
> **Average response:** Strongly agree.

The survey results showed that, on average, Liberty Hill parishioners strongly agreed with the statement that racism still exists but in different forms. Many parishioners expressed the belief that racism is a sinful aspect of humanity and that as long as sin is present, racism will persist in various forms. Their perspective conveyed the understanding that the key for believers is to activate the ministry of reconciliation and exemplify love to the world. This viewpoint emphasized an ongoing commitment to address racism in its evolving manifestations and the importance of embodying the principles of reconciliation and love within the Christian community.

> **Statement #11:** "I am uncomfortable doing ministry with an all-Caucasian church."
>
> **Average Response:** Strongly disagree.

The survey results indicated that, on average, Liberty Hill parishioners strongly disagreed with the statement suggesting discomfort in doing ministry with an all-Caucasian church. Parishioners at Liberty Hill Baptist Church expressed a notable level of comfort, with some responses indicating that the idea of doing ministry with an all-Caucasian church "does not bother [them] at all." This strong disagreement reflects a sense of openness and readiness among parishioners to engage in ministry with churches of different racial compositions, fostering an environment that promotes collaboration and unity in Christian service.

> **Statement #12:** "White Southern missionaries should stay in the South and minister in their context."
>
> **Average response:** Strongly disagree.

The survey results showed that, on average, Liberty Hill parishioners strongly disagreed with the statement suggesting that white Southern missionaries should stay in the South and minister in their context. Responses to this statement were often grounded in biblical principles and referenced the Great Commission as the foundation for doing ministry. The consensus among respondents reflected a belief in the universal call to spread the gospel without limitations based on geographical or racial boundaries. This understanding of the broader mission emphasized the idea that Christians, regardless of their background, are called to go and minister wherever the need arises, aligning with the teachings of Jesus in the Great Commission.

> **Statement #13:** "The Southern Baptist Convention is a diverse organization."
>
> **Average response:** Moderately disagree.

The survey results indicated that, on average, Liberty Hill parishioners moderately disagreed with the statement suggesting that the SBC is a diverse organization. Though the Southern Baptist Convention is predominately white, it is noteworthy that it is considered one of the most diverse conventions. The response to this statement likely reflects both an acknowledgment of the existing diversity within the SBC and an awareness of the predominant representation and the room for further inclusion and representation within the organization.

> **Statement #14:** "Jesus's sacrifice on the cross is the roadmap toward racial reconciliation."
>
> **Average response:** Strongly agree.

The survey results revealed that, on average, Liberty Hill parishioners strongly agreed with the statement asserting that Jesus's sacrifice on the cross is the road map toward racial reconciliation.

Members of Liberty Hill Baptist Church expressed a unified belief in the transformative power of the resurrection and the example Jesus set for his followers. The consensus emphasized not only an acknowledgment of Jesus's sacrifice but also a recognition of the challenge in translating that example into action. Despite this challenge, Liberty Hill parishioners affirmed their understanding that the ministry of reconciliation provided through the death, burial, and resurrection of Jesus Christ serves as a guiding force toward racial reconciliation.

> **Statement #15:** "An issued apology from the Southern Baptist Convention is not enough for the role played in slavery."
>
> **Average response:** Moderately agree.

The survey results showed that, on average, Liberty Hill parishioners moderately agreed with the statement expressing that an issued apology from the SBC is not enough for the role played in slavery. Though they acknowledged the significance of an apology as a starting point, respondents emphasized the need for continued actionable and progressive steps forward to accompany the apology. This response reflects a desire for tangible efforts and initiatives from the SBC, beyond a mere apology, to address the historical role played in slavery and actively contribute to healing and reconciliation. Part of reducing the noise is the ability to remain aligned with biblical standards despite the world's anxieties. Reflections from the results of a parishioner's survey evidenced a Christian perspective and represented the ability to reduce the noise and maintain God's perspective with each statement.

Statement #1: "Slavery impacts my relationship with Caucasians." Reflection: My relationship with my white brothers and sisters is not based on the history of slavery but on the history of Calvary. The death, burial, and resurrection of Jesus Christ releases people from the bondage of sin and allows restoration, forgiveness, and hope. Therefore, slavery does not impact my relationship with Caucasians. They are my brothers and sisters in Christ, and no matter what they do to me or what I do to them, I am called to love.

Statement #2: "Racial reconciliation is nice to pursue but will not be accomplished in my lifetime." Reflection: Reconciliation has already been accomplished. However, the question is, will we ask believers in Jesus Christ to walk in unity? Individuals who lack a personal relationship with Jesus Christ their Savior cannot truly grasp the depth of reconciliation. Racial reconciliation attempts grounded in earthly frameworks are inherently fragile. Therefore, a believer's wholehearted acceptance of reconciliation should serve as a catalyst for others to likewise embrace or encounter genuine reconciliation.

Statement #3: "Faith overrides flesh regarding my racial tendencies." Reflection: Acknowledging the universal struggle to live out faith daily, the reflection conveys that moments arise when human frailty becomes evident. The idea of "an eye for an eye," once approved in Lev 24:17–22, become reversed as Jesus speaks against this principle in Matt 5:38–48. Faith must override the flesh and allow a new conversation to capture one's mind and actions. Even in challenging times, the presence of the Holy Spirit provides the strength needed to persevere in walking by faith.

Statement #4: "If the Southern Baptist Convention changed its name, it would attract more African Americans." Reflection: Attracting more African Americans to a religious convention does not align with the teachings of the Bible. Changes in name alone do not bring growth; it is the Holy Spirit's work. If the SBC remains faithful in preaching and teaching the gospel of Jesus Christ, God will draw people of all races and ethnicities to himself. The only name of significance is the name of Jesus.

Statement #5: "White missionaries from the South have little to no impact doing ministry in urban areas." Reflection: This idea is baseless. If my white brothers and sisters are spreading the gospel message, they have every right and authority to do so. The impact should not be solely measured by the number of salvations; the very act of sharing the gospel is, in itself, a substantial impact. More Christian missionaries are needed in urban areas to saturate them with the gospel of Jesus Christ and offer the hope of salvation to the lost. The color of the messenger is irrelevant, as long as the message remains consistent, resulting in a significant impact.

Statement #6: "Workshops on racial reconciliation have little to no impact on racial reconciliation." Reflection: Everything mentioned in the previous reflection applies to this reflection. The only additional emphasis is on whether the workshop incorporates elements of the work of Jesus Christ. If the workshop only addresses the historical aspects of racial reconciliation, there will be minimal meaningful impact. However, if the workshop deeply emphasizes the power of Jesus Christ to transform hearts and minds, a notable impact can be expected, and lives will be changed.

Statement #7: "It is hard to forgive former Ku Klux Klan members for acts against African Americans." Reflection: Jesus Christ exemplified forgiveness and instructed his disciples to do the same. Although the question may appear challenging, I am confident that Christians can overcome any difficulty through obedience to God.

Statement #8: "The Southern Baptist Convention is a racist organization." Reflection: I hold the belief that the SBC planted detrimental seeds in America through its defense of slavery. However, labeling the SBC as a racist organization makes me uncomfortable, considering the evangelistic efforts associated with its membership. Characterizing the SBC as racist would imply that all Southern Baptists are racists, and that is an inaccurate assertion.

Statement #9: "Christians have not been a shining example of racial reconciliation." Reflection: If there is one area where Christians can improve, it is modeling the example of Jesus Christ to the world. Moreover, we as Christians have fallen short of being a shining example of racial reconciliation. Despite our segregated worship services, I do not believe we have yet been intentional about showing the world what racial unity looks like. While there are exceptions out there, the vast majority of churches can do a better job of being more intentional and strategic about showing love toward one another.

Statement #10: "Racism still exists but in different forms." Reflection: As long as there is sin in the world, racism will have a place to thrive. However, believers in Jesus Christ must follow the mandate of the Great Commission to make disciples who make disciples. In doing so, hatred decreases, and room for understanding and cooperation abounds.

Statement #11: "I am uncomfortable doing ministry with an all-Caucasian church." Reflection: This is not true in the least. I welcome opportunities to partner with my brothers and sisters in Christ, whether in worship services, mission trips, or prayer walks in the neighborhood.

Statement #12: "White Southern missionaries should stay in the South and minister in their context." Reflection: In an atmosphere where racism has been highlighted and discussed, this statement is outrageous and is undeserving of attention. If a church agrees with this statement, issues beyond race should be examined.

Statement #13: "The Southern Baptist Convention is a diverse organization." Reflection: While I am still determining the demographics of the SBC, I can assume that there is a percentage of diversity within it based on its sheer size.

Statement #14: "Jesus's sacrifice on the cross is the road map toward racial reconciliation." Reflection: The cross is enough. In many ways, the death, burial, and resurrection of Jesus Christ is taken for granted, thus limiting its power over worldly issues and matters of race. However, like Jesus, we must be willing to make sacrifices for racial unity and harmony within the world.

Statement #15: "An issued apology from the Southern Baptist Convention is not enough for the role played in slavery." Reflection: If the SBC had never apologized for the role they played in slavery, all is still forgiven because of the saving grace of Jesus Christ. While I am just learning about the apology issued by the SBC, I salute the convention for seeking reconciliation. One can never examine the heart of an apology. Therefore, taking things at face value, I can receive the apology and forgive in obedience to the command of our Savior Jesus Christ.

Reducing the noise means keeping external influences, events, and activities from silencing the voice of God in one's life. While others responded through their intellect or knowledge base, this survey represented someone who consciously chose to follow God's heartbeat. May like-minded believers find ways to reduce the external noise to respond in obedience to God's Word.

5

CAN WE REGAIN THE COURAGE?

The SBC seemed to lack courage during a critical point in American history. Despite the pressing need for spiritual leadership during a tumultuous period, the SBC adopted only one resolution addressing racial issues from 1961 to 1978. Southern Baptist leaders, along with the entire nation, were exposed to the resurgence of lynchings, church bombings, political assassinations, riots, educational imbalances, and increased police brutality. However, the lack of resolutions during a heated moment in American history disproved my hypothesis. In my presentation, I emphasized that the apparent disappearance of Southern Baptist resolutions should not overshadow the efforts from individuals and churches that exercised their autonomy to address injustices. Nevertheless, the convention remained relatively silent, and the scarcity of resolutions seemed to reflect a hesitancy to confront these challenges in subsequent years.

The parishioners of Liberty Hill Baptist Church paid heightened attention during this segment of my presentation, especially because many of them lived through the events of the 1960s as youth and young adults. Historical context was not a distant background for them; it was their lived experience. My mentor, Rev. Dr. Otis Moss Jr., and his wife, Edwina Hudson Moss, were active participants alongside Dr. Martin Luther King Jr. during the formative years of the civil rights movement. They vividly recalled the challenges of garnering support from religious leaders during those transformative times.

In the **Resolution on Meeting with National Baptist Negro Leaders—Louisville, Kentucky (1959)**, the messengers of the SBC acknowledged that internal anxieties were fueled by external forces, causing a significant disturbance that demanded attention and resolution.[1] This resolution brought attention to the "continuing existing tensions and pressures." However, rather than directly challenging pastors, leaders, and believing Christians to take a stance, the resolution recommended that "local, state, and state agencies and workers" should engage in a ministry of service and understanding with Christians of all races and nationalities. Finally, the resolution emphasized the importance of "the continued

[1] "Resolution on Meeting with National Baptist Negro Leaders," sbc.net, May 1, 1959, https://www.sbc.net/resource-library/resolutions/resolution-on-meeting-with-national-baptist-negro-leaders/.

prayerful and responsible application of the principles and example of Christ."

On the horizon, the civil rights movement was brewing, and leaders of the SBC acknowledged, in the **Resolution on Race Relations—St. Louis, Missouri (1961)**, "that members of their churches had sincere differences of opinion regarding the best course of action in this matter."[2] However, the language used in this resolution differed from that of the 1940s and 1950s. Earlier resolutions showed a confident resolve to settle issues concerning injustices, at least in ink. SBC messengers adopted resolutions that urged Southern Baptists to move beyond "merely writing, teaching, and praying against the lynchers, leaving the helpless and innocent victims of crime with no adequate or sufficient protection."[3] It is important to note that, though this resolution stands in history in readable form, it recognized the impactful role of the SBC as the largest Christian group with a keen sense of Christian responsibility. However, what had happened to the bold voices of messengers from the convention?

Despite the nation's upheaval, resolutions on communism, tax study, the American Bible Society, and a relief for progress in the Pacific coast area were passed. In 1963, the Baptist Faith and Message addressed many of the SBC's theological concerns. Other resolutions covered human freedom, messengers' spiritual right to engage society, federal public funds, and various acknowledgments

---

[2] "Resolution on Race Relations," sbc.net, June 1, 1961, https://www.sbc.net/resource-library/resolutions/resolution-on-race-relations-2/.

[3] "Hillyer Resolutions," sbc.net, May 1, 1906, https://www.sbc.net/resource-library/resolutions/hillyer-resolutions/.

and appreciations. In 1964, resolutions acknowledged the West Coast Laymen's Crusade and the American Bible Society and requested President Lyndon B. Johnson to appoint a commission to investigate the dangers of alcohol to public health. However, a worldwide tragedy occurred that received no attention in the resolutions, and Liberty Hill parishioners noticed.

On November 22, 1963, the thirty-fifth president of the United States, John Fitzgerald Kennedy, was assassinated. According to the John F. Kennedy Presidential Library and Museum, the initial rejection of Kennedy's candidacy was due to anti-Catholic biases.[4] Liberty Hill parishioners, remembering Kennedy's advocacy for the African American community, found it noteworthy that the SBC messengers did not issue a resolution acknowledging the president's assassination. While recognizing that the lack of a resolution does not necessarily imply a lack of condolences from Southern Baptist churches, members of Liberty Hill raised questions about why the convention issued resolutions on various matters, including the dangers of alcohol, but remained silent on the assassination of a globally esteemed United States president. The absence of resolutions led parishioners to engage in speculative thoughts.

In 1965, SBC messengers passed resolutions covering topics such as obscenity, church-state relations, the Sunday School Board, and Operation Penetration—a united effort to spread God's Word globally. Notably, a resolution on "Human Relations" acknowledged

---

[4] "John F. Kennedy and Religion," John F. Kennedy Presidential Library and Museum, https://www.jfklibrary.org/learn/about-jfk/jfk-in-history/john-f-kennedy-and-religion.

racial tensions, urging messengers to rededicate themselves to a Christlike ministry of reconciliation. Richard W. Luebbert proposed a more direct amendment, which expressed condemnation for using violence and bloodshed to influence legislation or societal changes.[5] This action demonstrated that despite the convention's overall silence in resolutions, there were still courageous messengers willing to address and support racial efforts during challenging moments in American history.

In 1966, the American Bible Society celebrated the 150th anniversary of its widespread distribution. During this year, the SBC messengers issued resolutions emphasizing the work of the American Bible Society and their printing campaign of the Word of God, and they urged state conventions, associations, and Southern Baptist churches to celebrate and contribute to their ongoing work. Additionally, resolutions were passed addressing Christian attitudes in the modern world, the Fellowship of Christian Athletes, the acknowledgment of Christian expansion in urban areas, and a peace resolution addressing the Vietnam War. Amidst a plethora of topics, including war, the sexual revolution, drug and alcohol consumption, and various theological concerns, racial issues were absent.[6] The extensive array of matters during this era raises the question of whether there were too many issues demanding attention to adequately address racial concerns.

---

[5] "Resolution On Human Relations," sbc.net, https://www.sbc.net/resource-library/resolutions/resolution-on-human-relations/.

[6] "Resources in Resolutions," sbc.net, https://www.sbc.net/resource-library/resolutions/?fwp_resolutions_by_year=1966-annual-meeting.

In 1967, a resolution on peace acknowledged military aggression and the wars in other nations. Southern Baptist messengers resolved to support elected leaders "in developing strong and wise policies" and maintaining order worldwide.[7] Resolutions also addressed the separation of church and state, the population explosion in America, and again, the American Bible Society, whose organization continued providing, without charge, Scriptures for distribution to men and women of the armed forces and patients in veterans hospitals. In 1968, the messengers of the SBC passed resolutions on alcohol, the crusades of the Americas, highway safety control, pornographic materials, church-state relations, and a congressional acknowledgment of the proper regard for Sunday as the Lord's Day.

On April 4, 1968, the Reverend Dr. Martin Luther King Jr. was shot outside the Lorraine Motel in Memphis, Tennessee. Members of Liberty Hill Baptist Church did not anticipate that there would be a Southern Baptist resolution, and they were correct. Although King's assassination was not acknowledged at the 1968 SBC annual meeting, the work he did benefited not only the African American community but all communities. According to one Liberty Hill parishioner, "The Southern Baptist Convention missed an opportunity." The conspicuous absence of a resolution or condolence for President John Fitzgerald Kennedy or for civil rights leader the Reverend Dr. Martin Luther King Jr. did not sit well with Liberty Hill parishioners, and due to the lack of response, parishioners formed their own opinions.

---

[7] "Resolution on Peace," sbc.net, https://www.sbc.net/resource-library/resolutions/resolution-on-peace-10/.

On June 6, 1968, Senator Robert Francis Kennedy entered the Ambassador Hotel's Embassy Ballroom in Los Angeles, California, to speak with campaign supporters.[8] After addressing the gathering, Kennedy left through the hotel's kitchen and was gunned down by Sirhan Sirhan, a Palestinian-Jordanian man. Senator Kennedy was pronounced dead at the Good Samaritan Hospital, and the nation mourned the assassination of another Kennedy. The SBC passed the 1968 **Resolution on Violence, Disregard for the Law**, which mentioned "the tragic death of Senator Kennedy" but was mainly a plea to Congress to pass gun laws.[9] During this silence, the Southern Baptist messengers "petitioned executive, legislative, and judicial leaders to uphold the law and take positive steps to establish a climate of respect for the law." Moreover, the resolution "called upon Baptist people to renew their allegiance to civil authority, respect the rights of others, and cooperate with all agencies responsible for maintaining law and order." Over time, the SBC reestablished their voice.

Reclaiming courage requires a readiness to confront and address race relations despite inherent challenges. Racial reconciliation can be likened to football, portrayed as a contact sport where gentle yards have no place and enduring hits is an integral part of the game. Those willing to withstand, rise after a hit, and persist

---

[8] The Associated Press, "How the AP Covered the RFK Assassination 50 Years Ago," June 4, 2018, https://www.ap.org/media-center/ap-in-the-news/2018/how-the-ap-covered-the-rfk-assassination-50-years-ago/.

[9] "Resolution On Violence, Disregard For Law", June 1, 1968, https://www.sbc.net/resource-library/resolutions/resolution-on-violence-disregard-for-law/.

in the journey will eventually make progress, much like scoring a touchdown in football. Kevin and Penny Litchfield, former directors of missions for the Cleveland Hope association in Cleveland, Ohio, serve as exemplars who comprehended and embraced the demanding nature of the contact sport of racial reconciliation. Their dedication to God and willingness to confront challenges made them not only passionate leaders but also cherished friends. The lasting impact of the Litchfields' sacrifices in northeast Ohio will resonate for years, with one example standing out among their many courageous acts.

In the face of challenges such as abandoned buildings, dilapidated houses, unemployment, poverty, and crime in Cleveland, the Litchfields envisioned taking action. With the support of willing missionaries and the backing of the Southern Baptist community, they embarked on the transformation of a run-down duplex in a predominantly black neighborhood. One side was used for their family, and the other was designated for visiting missionaries. This initiative, fueled by a profound sense of commitment and love, demanded a substantial investment from their life savings. The neighborhood, previously characterized by criminal activity and neglect, became a focal point for positive change. Kevin believed in making a meaningful impact, and as missionaries engaged in activities like planting flowers, maintaining the landscape, and understanding the community's needs, the visual perception of the neighborhood began to shift. The Mission House turned into a welcoming space for local families and for hosting picnics, fun activities, and Bible studies. Additionally, missionaries from various parts of the country lived in the Mission House during summers, actively serving the community.

During these positive transformations, the community's darker aspects surfaced. The Mission House and the Litchfield family experienced frequent break-ins, one of which occurred while the family slept at night. Concerns about the safety of the Litchfields were widespread. Despite facing these challenges, Kevin held on to his courage, grounded in the understanding that the work in that area was dedicated to the glory of God rather than personal gain. Enduring property damage, sleepless nights, and compromised safety, Kevin persisted in serving and loving a black community that, at times, kept him at arm's length. The resilience to continue serving was anchored in one purpose: the will of God. Regaining courage, in this context, was not centered on the individual but on fulfilling a higher purpose, even if it caused negative consequences. However, one day Kevin encountered an African American male near his home. This was not just any man; it was the man who controlled the neighborhood. Following their interaction, the man assured Kevin that his house would not be broken into again, and indeed, it was not. The Litchfields subsequently joined Liberty Hill Baptist Church, becoming the only white family in a predominantly black congregation. Despite his responsibilities as director of missions, Kevin and his family remained courageous and played a crucial role in assisting church leadership in navigating the complexities of the SBC.

Despite the historical disappointments with resolutions, or the lack thereof, from the SBC messengers, the late 1970s witnessed a noticeable shift as a consistent flow of resolutions demonstrated a desire for the SBC to deepen its connection with and support for its minority population. **The Resolution on Racism—Atlanta, Georgia (1978)** marked a turning point by acknowledging the progress of the civil rights movement and expressing lament for discrimination in job opportunities and housing for minorities.[10] The convention made a resolution to "purge ourselves and our society of all forms of racism." The use of the phrase "purge ourselves" indicated an acknowledgment of challenges within the convention, and there appeared to be a commitment "to applying the teachings of Jesus to address the practical concerns of all minority individuals." The inclusion of biblical references in the resolutions underscored the messengers' intention to ground their calls for action in God's Word. The **Declaration of Human Rights—Atlanta, Georgia (1978)** stands out for its uniqueness in adding actionable items to the resolutions. Rooted in Scripture, this resolution emphasized the significance of demonstrating Christian values to the world. The action items included a commitment to political action on behalf of human rights, a call to preach the Word without fear or favor, an encouragement for Southern Baptist churches to boldly champion justice for the oppressed, and an emphasis on Baptist agencies remaining uncompromised in their commitment to human rights.

The **Resolution on Black and Ethnic Involvement—Pittsburgh, Pennsylvania (1983)** marked a shift in the Southern

---

[10] "Resolution on Racism," sbc.net, June 1, 1978, https://www.sbc.net/resource-library/resolutions/resolution-on-racism/.

Baptists' focus toward including a broader group of minorities.[11] Encompassing over five thousand churches from Alaska to Puerto Rico, churches that represented black and ethnic communities and covered eighty languages, the SBC sought to broaden its engagement with minority groups. The pulpit abilities and administrative capabilities of leaders in these ethnic communities allowed ministries to stay indigenous and fruitful. With that in mind, the SBC leadership believed it was in the best interest of the convention to involve these leaders in places of responsible leadership. The resolution states, "We encourage all agencies, boards, and committees to seek out ethnic and black leadership from within the Southern Baptist family . . . to serve on boards, committees, commissions, and programs of the Southern Baptist Convention so as to reflect more completely the oneness in Christ and a stronger influence for our Lord everywhere and with everyone." Leadership inclusion showed a step toward racial reconciliation that Liberty Hill parishioners acknowledged despite past transgressions. Although far from redemption, Southern Baptist messengers acknowledged the gifts and talents of its minority members and sought ways to include them in leadership roles.

The **Resolution on Involvement of Blacks and Other Minorities in Southern Baptist Convention Life—Atlanta, Georgia (1986)** acknowledges that "Blacks and other minorities have been an integral part of the Southern Baptist Convention since

---

[11] "Resolution On Black And Ethnic Involvement," sbc.net, June 1, 1983, https://www.sbc.net/resource-library/resolutions/resolution-on-black-and-ethnic-involvement/.

its organization in 1845."[12] This resolution took some liberty with the participation of blacks and minorities since the convention's founding. However, the willingness to "allow its members to express themselves from their ethnic-cultural heritage" is well documented. The messengers "encourage its agencies and committees to increase the involvement of blacks and other minorities in employment, missions, and programs." By the 1980s, the resolutions of the SBC went beyond participation and encouraged leadership and planning to those gifted minority leaders and administrators. The significance of this resolution cannot be overstated, as Southern Baptists sought to be more inclusive and seek racial harmony and peace.

[12] "Resolution On Involvement Of Blacks And Other Minorities In Southern Baptist Convention Life," sbc.net, June 1, 1986, https://www.sbc.net/resource-library/resolutions/resolution-on-involvement-of-blacks-and-other-minorities-in-southern-baptist-convention-life/

6

Can We Rediscover the Cross?

The salvific significance of the resurrection is unquestionable in Christian theology. For believers, the Romans Road serves as a guide to eternity, with Rom 3:23 underscoring the universal human condition of sin, stating that "all have sinned and fall short of the glory of God." This verse emphasizes the inherent fallen nature of humanity and the need for redemption.

The consequences of sin are highlighted in Rom 6:23, which states that "the wages of sin is death." Despite the seemingly enticing nature of sin, it carries a heavy cost. However, the verse also introduces the concept of God's gift of eternal life through Jesus Christ, providing a way to be reconciled with God. The pivotal role of Jesus's death, burial, and resurrection is expounded upon in the Christian message. Jesus, by sacrificing himself on the cross, offers forgiveness of sins and the opportunity for believers to be reconciled with God the Father. Romans 10:9 extends an invitation to unbelievers, urging them to confess their belief in the Lord Jesus and acknowledge his resurrection, thus becoming believers.

In the context of the black church, the song "No Greater Love" by David Allen holds particular significance. Often sung during Easter, the song narrates the story of Jesus's death, burial, and resurrection. Its powerful lyrics and melody evoke strong emotions, leading to raised hands, tears, and shouts of praise. The song becomes a poignant expression of love, emphasizing the sacrificial nature of Jesus's act on the cross. However, to fully grasp the depth of this love, believers must journey back to the crucifixion to understand the profound significance of Jesus's death. Before pursuing racial reconciliation, one must delve into the profound messages conveyed at Calvary. The death of Jesus, a pinnacle "actions speak louder than words" moment, encapsulates a deeper truth. Despite the prevalent discourse on racial reconciliation, there is a frustration that mere talk, lectures, teaching, and preaching fall short of genuine sacrifice.

While primarily addressing salvation, the death of Jesus embodies a love that the world may misconstrue. A pivotal aspect of this love is Jesus's act of forgiveness even in the face of extreme adversity. Before Jesus breathed his last breath on Calvary's cross, he astonishingly requested forgiveness for his abusers. This request, however, was made possible because Jesus had already forgiven them. This act of forgiveness raises the question, If Jesus could forgive his abusers and urged his followers to do the same, why do many Christians struggle with forgiveness? The difficulty in forgiveness often lies in the context of the situation. Consider the circumstances surrounding Jesus: he was lied about, physically abused, spat upon, dragged up a hill, nailed to a cross, and subjected to taunts. Despite this, Jesus forgave. Reflecting on this context challenges Christians to confront their own struggles with forgiveness and encourages a deeper understanding of the transformative power of forgiveness in the pursuit of racial reconciliation.

The context provided is powerful. Jesus, while on the verge of death on the cross, maintained compassion for his abusers, extending forgiveness even as he engaged heaven. By doing this Jesus prompts a crucial question for his followers: Is it possible to forgive those who have trespassed against you? Moreover, given the historical relationship between blacks and whites, can the black church forgive the profound evils of slavery, lynching, prejudices, racist acts, church bombings, water hoses, police dog bites, billy club hits, name-calling, and other heinous acts that have marginalized and pushed communities to the fringes? Responses from many parishioners at Liberty Hill Baptist Church reflected a complex sentiment, acknowledging the possibility of forgiveness while also expressing a significant "but." Engaging in an honest conversation about the challenge of following the example of Jesus revealed deep pain among Liberty Hill members and unearthed layers of racial reconciliation that had not been previously confronted. The pain runs deep, making it profoundly difficult to forgive the historical traumas of the black experience. It becomes a unique pain corresponding to the inability of Gentiles to fully comprehend the depth of the Jewish Holocaust. Yet amid this struggle, there was a wrestling among Liberty Hill parishioners when they learned that the SBC had done something unexpected: issued an apology. This acknowledgment opened a new avenue for discussion and reflection on the possibility of reconciliation within the broader context of the Southern Baptist community.

The **Resolution on Racial Reconciliation on the 150th Anniversary of the Southern Baptist Convention—Atlanta, Georgia (1995)** served as both the inspiration for this book and a powerful challenge to confront the racist history attributed to the SBC.[1] The language employed in the resolution to articulate past transgressions indicated a genuine acknowledgment from SBC messengers of the need to seek, in their words, repentance, forgiveness, and reconciliation with the African American population within the convention. While the saying "actions speak louder than words" holds weight, the words chosen in this resolution spoke volumes and presented a crucial starting point for racial reconciliation. When I presented this information to the members of Liberty Hill Baptist Church, I anticipated a range of reactions, from surprise to shock, as they encountered the unexpected admission of guilt, repentance, forgiveness, and hope for the future expressed by Southern Baptist messengers in this historic resolution.

The resolution begins by recognizing the effectiveness of Southern Baptists as "instruments of God in missions, evangelism, and social ministry." Despite Liberty Hill parishioners' feelings toward the SBC's past, this resolution acknowledged the undeniable role it played in taking the gospel worldwide, a mission emphasized by the convention's earliest messengers through the Foreign

---

[1] "Resolution On Racial Reconciliation On The 150th Anniversary Of The Southern Baptist Convention," sbc.net, June 1, 1995, https://www.sbc.net/resource-library/resolutions/resolution-on-racial-reconciliation-on-the-150th-anniversary-of-the-southern-baptist-convention/.

Mission Board. However, the resolution takes a significant shift by addressing the pain experienced by the African American population within the SBC. It explicitly states, "Our relationship to African-Americans has been hindered from the beginning by the role that slavery played in the formation of the Southern Baptist Convention." This acknowledgment resonated deeply with members of Liberty Hill Baptist Church, as it demonstrated a willingness to confront a part of history often overlooked or glossed over. Continuing, the resolution openly admits that "Southern Baptist forebears defended the right to own slaves, and either participated in, supported, or acquiesced in a particular inhumane nature of American slavery." This candid recognition of the convention's historical involvement in and support of slavery marks a crucial step toward understanding and addressing the past. The acknowledgment of this painful history is essential for fostering genuine reconciliation and healing within the SBC.

As this part of the presentation unfolded, I paused to allow members of Liberty Hill Baptist Church time to process the information. The impact of the resolution's language became evident as I observed shifts in the reactions of the onlookers. Expressions of surprise, such as hands on the sides of faces, squinting of eyes, and audible sounds of exhalation, conveyed a sense that something unexpected had transpired. The parishioners had not anticipated gathering to hear an acknowledgment from the SBC regarding the wrongs of its past. I intentionally projected each resolution on the screen to allow the attendees to visually engage with the words and sentiments expressed. The admission of the hindrance caused by slavery in the formation and relations of the SBC prompted a period of silence among Liberty Hill parishioners. One parishioner's statement, "I didn't know they said all that," highlighted what a revelation it was to learn that the SBC had candidly acknowledged its historical role.

A key objective of the presentation was to inform parishioners about various ways the SBC has sought racial reconciliation. If they did not understand these efforts, it would be difficult for Liberty Hill members to form a comprehensive and informed perspective on the SBC. If parishioners were going to have a pessimistic view of the SBC, it would be better for them to do so with all the information. While the information presented in this resolution may not have immediately swayed parishioners' opinions about the SBC, the essential point is that exposure to this information is crucial for forming perspectives. It is important to emphasize that this resolution does not diminish the commendable work done by individual churches, entities, boards, or Southern Baptists who actively participated in promoting justice and equality during the civil rights movement. However, as a collective voice of the SBC, this resolution serves as a candid acknowledgment of historical wrongs.

Continuing with its acknowledgments, the resolution highlights the follies of some Southern Baptists who "failed, in many cases, to support, and in some cases opposed, legitimate initiatives to secure the civil rights of African-Americans." The significance of this admission cannot be understated, as it marked a turning point in history, had a profound impact on associations, and identified the cause of significant fractures in relationships within the body of Christ. The failure to support civil rights initiatives for African Americans is recognized as having contributed to "discrimination, oppression, injustice, and violence, both in the Civil War and throughout the history of our nation." This indifference on the part of the SBC is acknowledged to have resulted in detrimental consequences, not only causing suffering within the body of Christ but also leading to a significant separation within the SBC from "our African-American brothers and sisters." The resolution thus addresses the severe impact of historical failures on both the broader societal context and the internal unity of the SBC.

As I encouraged open discussion, the weight of the information seemed to envelop the members of Liberty Hill Baptist Church in contemplative silence. The significance of the SBC's acknowledgment, made before a large audience of nearly fifteen thousand people, became a topic of national media discourse. Various news outlets presented diverse perspectives on the resolution, some suggesting it was an effort to attract African Americans into what was perceived as a declining convention. However, it is plausible that the messengers aimed to extend an olive branch to the African American community within the SBC and invite others to join. The resolution not only delved into the acknowledgment of the slave years and inactivity but also recognized the peril of the church's resistance to accept African Americans in their fellowship, stating that it "profoundly distorts our understanding of Christian morality, leading some Southern Baptists to believe that racial prejudice and discrimination are incompatible with the Gospel."

The resolution effectively addresses the root of racism by delving into a less discussed aspect—its biblical ramifications that can mislead people. By concluding with the sacrificial role of Jesus, who offered reconciliation through his death, burial, and resurrection, the resolution sets a tone of redemption, oneness, and unity. After first acknowledging the various acts of evil perpetrated against marginalized communities, the SBC messengers shift their focus to the resolutions outlined in the document. First, the messengers "denounce racism in all its forms as a deplorable sin." This statement carries a strong moral stance against any manifestation of racism. Next, there is an affirmation of the Christian principle of the inherent value and equality of all individuals. Furthermore, the messengers "lament and repudiate historic acts of evil such as slavery, acknowledging the ongoing consequences of these past injustices that continue to affect society." The resolution recognizes the need to confront and address the lasting impact of historical atrocities like slavery.

Liberty Hill parishioners found solace in reading the documented confession from the messengers of the SBC but grappled with the unsettling reality that multiple generations had benefited from the atrocious acts being apologized for. Liberty Hill parishioners grappled mentally with a history that spanned numerous generations, aware that their known ancestors endured the oppression that current messengers benefit from today—ancestors who survived an abhorrent journey on slave ships, weathered the horrors of slavery, lived through the Civil War, fought for justice during the civil rights movement, withstood periods of lynchings, and faced discrimination all while navigating the challenges of raising families, seeking employment, providing sustenance, and maintaining hope for a brighter future. Given this complex history, accepting mere words from a resolution proved challenging for Liberty Hill parishioners. I facilitated a platform for parishioners to share their concerns and emotions. While some members found solace in the resolution's apology for "condoning and/or perpetuating individual and systemic racism," others, despite their faith journey, struggled to accept it because of past experiences. The resolution humbly requested forgiveness "from our African-American brothers and sisters," recognizing that the healing of the SBC itself was at stake. Reverend Gary Frost, the second vice president of the denomination, officially accepted the apology from the messengers of the SBC on behalf of African Americans.[2]

The Resolution on African-American Theological Education—Atlanta, Georgia (1995) expressed remorse for past discrimination and acknowledged the collaborative educational efforts that began in 1913 when the National Convention of Colored Baptists sought to establish a theological seminary for black Baptist preachers, an initiative that emerged during a period of "racial discrimination when African American students were barred from enrolling in Convention-supported seminaries."[3] Despite this historical context, by 1995, an increasing number of African American students were attending all SBC seminaries.

The **Resolution on the Arson of African-American Churches—New Orleans, Louisiana (1996)** was a response to a disturbing wave of violence targeting African American churches

---

[2] John Dart, "Southern Baptists Vote to Issue Apology for Past Racism," *The Los Angeles Times*, June 21, 1995, https://www.latimes.com /archives/la-xpm-1995-06-21-mn-15534-story.html.

[3] "Resolution On African-American Theological Education," sbc.net, June 1, 1995, https://www.sbc.net/resource-library/resolutions/resolution-on-african-american-theological-education/.

across the nation.[4] In the span of eighteen months, approximately thirty African American churches fell victim to destructive acts of arson. SBC messengers, recognizing the prevailing racism and discrimination in society, articulated their concerns through this resolution. They emphasized the church's role as society's most effective tool to reach reconciliation, aligning with biblical principles. Southern Baptists sought to foster unity within the Christian faith by affirming "that racial bigotry in all its forms is absolutely contrary to the tenets of biblical Christianity, and attacks against any church constitute an attack against the entire community." Resolutions like these aimed to ground Southern Baptists' responses in biblical justification and serve as rallying cries for Christians.

The messengers of the SBC condemned the arsons as "despicable and abominable acts of lawlessness and racism." Through this resolution, messengers acknowledged a commitment to racial reconciliation in communities heavily affected by violence against churches. The SBC messengers called upon "local, state, and federal governments to investigate these hate crimes promptly and vigorously." They fully urged the apprehension and prosecution of those responsible for these "cowardly acts of bigotry." Reflecting on this part of the presentation required Liberty Hill Baptist Church members to process their thoughts and emotions as they received information about the SBC. Rediscovering the significance of the cross of Jesus Christ becomes challenging in the face

---

[4] "Resolution on the Arson of African-American Churches," sbc.net, June 1, 1996, https://www.sbc.net/resource-library/resolutions/resolution-on-the-arson-of-african-american-churches/.

of an acknowledgement of wrongs, repentance, and an apology. For believers, the cross illustrates the depth of Jesus's love, as he forgave his abusers without an issued apology. In the case of the SBC messengers, nearly fifteen thousand people publicly apologized, through a resolution, for the wrongs against African Americans.

During discussions with one parishioner, an authentic conversation emerged about the acceptance of the Southern Baptist apology. The parishioner questioned, "Pastor, am I letting Southern Baptists off the hook if I accept this apology?" At the time of the presentation to Liberty Hill Baptist Church members, 172 years had passed, and this parishioner felt the "benefits of slavery, racism, and discrimination had been one-sided." The complexity of the question was nuanced. In response to the parishioner's questioning, I listened and offered an understanding ear. A complexity of emotions emerged as some members of Liberty Hill Baptist Church grappled with the significance of the cross of Jesus Christ. For a few members, the example of Jesus in the face of his abusers began to overshadow their human instincts, and the possibility of accepting and forgiving started to seem feasible. However, others among the parishioners were not ready to embrace the cross so quickly, contending that the absence of slavery, racism, and discrimination would have fundamentally reshaped the economy, restored family units, opened opportunities, and created a different outcome for African Americans. Rediscovering the cross, in their view, meant more than simply understanding the details of the sacrifice Jesus made; it required a spiritual maturity that permeates the life of a believer.

As the pastor, I refrained from providing immediate answers to the questions posed by Liberty Hill parishioners. Instead, I listened attentively, recognizing the deeply personal connection associated with their individual journeys toward racial reconciliation. While external sources can offer crucial information, the individual must grapple with his or her response and subsequent actions upon acquiring such knowledge. Biblical texts such as "as we also have forgiven our debtors" (Matt 6:12b) resonate powerfully until one is faced with the challenge of extending forgiveness to those who trespass. Similarly, the biblical injunctions to "love your enemies" (Matt 5:44a) and "pray for those who persecute you" (Matt 5:44b) may seem lofty ideals until the moment arrives to practice them. The phrase "Father, forgive them, because they do not know what they are doing" (Luke 23:34), exemplified by Jesus, might be inspiring, but for many believers, embodying such forgiveness is an arduous task. The journey toward racial reconciliation resembles a winding freeway with off-ramps, detours, and rest stops. Some find the drive well lit with blue skies and sunshine, while others navigate through foggy conditions with gray skies and rain. Nevertheless, the essence of rediscovering the cross lies in the commitment of believers in Jesus Christ. Despite the challenges, the cross serves as a beacon of hope at the intersection where faith and life collide.

The **Resolution on Racial Reconciliation on the 150th Anniversary of the Southern Baptist Convention—Atlanta, Georgia (1995)** emerged as a pivotal step toward racial harmony and was considered a necessary starting point.[5] However, skeptics speculate that the resolution was a strategic response to a declining

[5] "Resolution On Racial Reconciliation on the 150th Anniversary of the Southern Baptist Convention."

SBC membership, with the goal of attracting more minority pastors and churches. But research suggests otherwise—a perspective I shared with the members of Liberty Hill. Despite the skepticism, Southern Baptist messengers persisted in their efforts to acknowledge historical wrongs. The **Resolution on the 150th Anniversary of the Dred Scott Decision—San Antonio, Texas (2007)** commemorated the notorious Dred Scott Decision by the United States Supreme Court.[6] This decision infamously declared that individuals "of African ancestry and their descendants had no rights which the white man was bound to respect, essentially denying them personhood and the right of citizenship." The SBC messengers affirmed the principles of the Declaration of Independence and recognized the role of key historical events, such as the 1863 Emancipation Proclamation, the 1954 *Brown v. Board* Supreme Court ruling, and the 1964 Civil Rights Act, in overturning the Dred Scott Decision.

Moreover, the messengers acknowledged their "complicity in this erroneous Supreme Court decision, admitting that when they failed to love, minister to, and share the Gospel with people based on their ethnicity, ability, or station in life, they were complicit." The Resolution Committee of the SBC also recognized the historic significance of the 1995 resolution, which "unreservedly denounced racism in all its forms as a deplorable sin" and affirmed the sanctity and equal worth of every human life, "made in God's image, irrespective of race or ethnicity." The external voices often serve as

---

[6] "Resolution on 150th Anniversary of the Dred Scott Decision," sbc.net, June 1, 2007, https://www.sbc.net/resource-library/resolutions/on-the-150th-anniversary-of-the-dred-scott-decision/.

distractions from the core message of the cross. In a world filled with diverse opinions and ongoing discriminatory acts, there is a concerted effort to divert attention away from the central theme of the cross. The cross serves as the ultimate guide for racial reconciliation, representing a focal point that is despised by the adversary of God and sometimes overlooked by believers who are still growing in their faith. While members of Liberty Hill Baptist Church could recite Scriptures from the Bible, I observed a reluctance among some to fully embrace the teachings of those Scriptures, particularly regarding the pursuit of reconciliation.

Matthew 5:44 implores followers of Jesus Christ to love their enemies and pray for those who mistreat them. Despite the recognition of this Scripture, some individuals merely acknowledge it, while others may dismiss it, displaying a level of spiritual immaturity even after spending their entire lives in the church. Jesus, through his actions, set an unparalleled example of forgiveness. However, there exists a paradox in which some individuals who profess love for the Lord struggle to extend that love to brothers and sisters of different races. The cross serves as a profound symbol, revealing the hearts of believers and presenting a collective challenge for the entire body of Christ. Reflecting on whether Jesus loves the little children of the world while witnessing a lack of love among people of different colors raises poignant questions. Perhaps the church has not been adequately challenged to embody forgiveness, love, sacrifice, and selflessness toward one another. The early church modeled these virtues even if it cost them their lives, and in many cases, it did.

Are there exceptions to forgiveness that were overlooked in Sunday school class? Are there conditional clauses to contemplate when accepting apologies from individuals or groups that acknowledge wrongdoing, express repentance, and seek forgiveness? Are slavery, racism, and discrimination outside of God's redemption plan? These questions are pivotal in the process of rediscovering the cross and demand thoughtful responses from believers who claim to follow Jesus Christ. When I presented this challenge to members of Liberty Hill, there was resistance. Do ego, stubbornness, and a selective application of the commands of Jesus Christ influence the decision on how and when to forgive? The cost of true discipleship, of following Jesus, entails surrendering oneself to him in a manner that honors the sacrifice he made on the cross. By extending that same grace to others, we rediscover the significance of the cross.

7

Can We Reclaim the Mission?

The imperative to embrace racial reconciliation within the framework of the Great Commission carries profound significance. The Great Commission should serve as the believer's primary motive for pursuing racial reconciliation. Reclaiming the mission entails setting aside personal agendas to wholeheartedly pursue the divine assignment that Jesus imparted to his followers. With unmatched authority and power, Jesus commissioned his disciples to go and make disciples by spreading the gospel message (Matt 28:18–20). This mandate does not endorse segregation, discrimination, or ostracism but advocates for unity in service of a cause that transcends individual preferences, cultures, races, or ethnicities. Uniting under the banner of the Great Commission offers believers a unique and invigorating experience.

In John 13:35, Jesus imparted a simple yet profound way for believers to demonstrate their discipleship—by loving one another. When the body of Christ actively loves, encourages, forgives, and reconciles with one another, it paints a vivid picture of unity in a world yearning to see faith lived out authentically. As I delved deeper into my presentation to the Liberty Hill members, I simultaneously found myself gearing up for the endeavor of planting a church. Though initially not inclined to take on such a task, the compelling need within our community, particularly among young African American men facing despair, became too evident to ignore. In 2015, I grappled with the challenge of convincing myself that I lacked the time and mental bandwidth for church planting, considering my existing commitments as the pastor of a sizable traditional African American church, ongoing doctoral studies at New Orleans Baptist Theological Seminary, service as chaplain to Major League Baseball's Cleveland Indians (now Guardians), and the responsibilities of a husband and father. Nevertheless, spurred on by the encouragement of my family and some Liberty Hill members, I embraced the challenge of planting a church to bring hope and inspiration to the youth in my neighborhood.

In 2010, upon joining the SBC, my appreciation for the Cooperative Program deepened significantly. This unified giving plan, involving thousands of churches, demonstrates how diverse congregations can collaborate to support worldwide ministry and missions. As a member of the SBC, Liberty Hill Baptist Church established an annual giving percentage scale that increased each year to contribute to the Cooperative Program. One of the recipients of the Cooperative Program is the North American Mission

Board, an entity of the SBC that trains, equips, and empowers church planters across North America. The theme presented and preached by Kevin Ezell, the president of the North American Mission Board, resonated deeply with me during 2014: "Whatever It Takes." This theme served as a catalyst, pulling me out of a dormant state and prompting me to employ a tool previously used solely for entertainment and profit: basketball. Basketball became the conduit for sharing the gospel message, building relationships, connecting with new individuals, and building community bonds. After engaging in basketball sessions within the neighborhood for a few months, word spread that I was a pastor.

On a memorable day, I drove toward the basketball hoop with the intention of executing a slam dunk. To my surprise, the defender leaped to block my shot, unaware of my background as a professional player in Europe. Needless to say, he was left embarrassed. I vividly remember dunking the basketball on him with such force that he fell to the ground. As I landed, the entire gym erupted in screams. I could hear numerous people expressing their surprise, with comments like "I didn't know pastors could dunk." This moment became transformative in the community as it defied their expectations—a pastor actively engaging in basketball. Although I gained approval within the basketball community, attending church remained a low priority for them. When I inquired about their reluctance to visit the church, I was told they liked me personally but "didn't like the whole church thing." Curious, I asked, "What does church look like to you?" They responded, "We play basketball, and you preach at halftime." It was at that moment I recalled Kevin Ezell's phrase, "Whatever It Takes." Subsequently, after discussions with my director of missions, I embarked on the journey of planting a church.

Embarking on the journey of church planting, I was acutely aware of my lack of experience in this domain. While I had observed my father and grandfather navigate the challenges of traditional churches, I recognized that planting a church presented its own unique set of obstacles. The endeavor entailed not only crafting weekly sermons but also addressing aspects such as vision, planning, strategizing, demographic reports, annual reports, partnerships, insurance, leadership teams, property, and a myriad of other priorities. Despite my familiarity with traditional pastoral roles, venturing into church planting required additional support. The North American Mission Board proved instrumental in this regard, offering a comprehensive guide for success. It provided a platform where leaders of diverse backgrounds could come together, offering mutual support. Through assessments, training programs, and mentorship opportunities, the North American Mission Board equipped me with the tools to build a leadership team and connect with potential church planters across the nation.

Balancing the role of a pastor in a traditional African American church while simultaneously launching a new church may seem challenging, but it was a strategic approach aimed at sharing the gospel with my community. This endeavor provided an active engagement with the SBC and helped foster unity between a predominantly black church and a predominantly white convention. After months of training, assessments, and team building, Encourage Church was successfully launched. Managing an 8:00 a.m. and an 11:00 a.m. worship service at Liberty Hill Baptist Church meant that the only feasible time for the new church plant was on Sundays from 3:00 to 5:00 p.m. This schedule allowed me to have lunch, change clothes, and set up for Encourage Church alongside my family.

Credit is due to Liberty Hill for not perceiving Encourage Church as a threat but rather as an extension of ministry needed in the community. Some parishioners actively collaborated, offering support in setup, greeting guests, and working with youth. Located within the East Professional Building, formerly East High School, the facility had been repurposed for the administrative functions of Cleveland Public Schools following a gymnasium roof collapse. After I had knocked on close to 350 neighborhood doors, it became evident that family-friendly activities were in demand, especially during the cold falls and frigid winters. Mothers and grandmothers emphasized the importance of providing youth with alternatives to keep them off the streets. To effectively meet these needs, Encourage Church had to embrace innovation and creativity. Encourage Church had its inaugural launch on January 3, 2016, featuring the impactful film *War Room*. Leveraging word-of-mouth promotions and the Liberty Hill radio broadcast, we achieved a commendable turnout for our church plant's debut. Despite the grandeur of a massive screen and a 900-seat auditorium, Encourage Church left a positive impression on Cleveland community attendees, showcasing Christ's love. Week after week, our team engaged in ministry through refreshments, brief talks, Lifeway movie series, and recreational activities for kids.

In the third month, a significant turning point occurred. While I was conducting a session, my wife informed me of a gathering in the gymnasium. Young men from the community, attracted by word of our activities, had decided to visit, not for the teaching session but for basketball games in the gymnasium. Recognizing the opportunity, I swiftly changed into sports attire and joined the basketball games. Over the subsequent four months, I witnessed how basketball served as a catalyst, opening doors to share the gospel, minister to youth, support the community, and teach me not to put limitations on God. As the numbers continued to grow, it became evident that additional support was necessary, especially as young men started traveling from other towns to participate in the basketball competitions. High school, college, and professional athletes engaged each week, not only in the sport but also in hearing the gospel message. Without formal advertising, Encourage Church experienced a surge in attendance and required additional assistance.

Over the course of a year, missionaries, pastors, and church leaders from the SBC visited from across the nation to witness the transformative work in our city. Churches formed partnerships, offered financial support, donated basketballs, covered referee expenses, and funded uniforms. Leaders journeyed from states like Texas, Georgia, North Carolina, Tennessee, and South Carolina, contributing prayers and resources to support our ministry to the community. The Great Commission was actively exercised through physical exercise, and souls were touched by the gospel message. The most gratifying aspect was witnessing black and white Christians working together to make a positive impact on the Cleveland area. Leaders did not just tour the city; they engaged in prayer walks, participated in beautification projects for homes, shared the gospel, and exemplified the joy of the Lord. Southern Baptist missionaries, representing various ages and nationalities, could observe God at work and were eager to offer their support. The Great Commission served as a powerful bond, connecting Liberty Hill parishioners and Southern Baptist messengers in a way that no other endeavor could achieve.

This eagerness to share the gospel paved the way for church-planting training, partnerships with other churches, and visits from missionaries; these interactions then created opportunities for multicultural fellowships, worship services, conversations, and relationships. The initiatives taken by the SBC aligned with its resolutions and showcased a commitment to invest in African American affairs. The Great Commission acted as a unifying force, bringing believers of all races together and gradually fostering unity, love, and mutual respect. Moreover, the Bible remained the driving force for unity and hope for communities. Resolutions in the 2000s maintained biblical standards while recognizing monumental events, and they coupled these standards with biblical expectations. The **Resolution on President Barack Hussein Obama—Louisville, Kentucky (2009)** coincided with the nation's celebration and division during the election of the first African American US president, Barack Obama.[1] SBC messengers, recognizing the historical impact of the institutional racism that had plagued America for centuries, expressed the "nation's pride in our continuing progress toward racial reconciliation" with the election of the forty-fourth president of the

[1] "Resolution on President Barack Hussein Obama," sbc.net, June 1, 2009, https://www.sbc.net/resource-library/resolutions/on-president-barack-hussein-obama/.

United States. While commending President Obama for his commitment to family, notably his love for First Lady Michelle Obama and their two daughters, Malia and Sasha, the resolution remained aligned with Southern Baptists' biblical values. The messengers of the Southern Baptist Convention voiced their opposition to various aspects of the new administration, including the "increase in funding for pro-abortion groups," the removal of "conscience protections" for pro-life healthcare professionals, and the declaration of June as Lesbian, Gay, Bisexual, and Transgender Pride Month. Across a spectrum of issues, such as foreign policies, responses to terrorist attacks, military strength, federal funding, abortion, and the preservation of the nation's Judeo-Christian heritage, the SBC messengers expressed a readiness to provide counsel and support to the new administration, emphasizing their commitment to biblical principles. Regardless of individual votes, the Southern Baptist messengers approached the resolution with cultural sensitivity and adherence to biblically sound perspectives.

The **Resolution on African American Contributions to American Baptist History—New Orleans (2012)** continued the pattern of recognizing and honoring the role of African Americans in shaping Baptist history in the United States.[2] Convention messengers acknowledged the historical oversights in the documentation of African American Baptist contributions throughout American history, and they expressed gratitude for the valuable

---

[2] "Resolution on African American Contributions to American Baptist History," sbc.net, June 1, 2012, https://www.sbc.net/resource-library/resolutions/on-african-american-contributions-to-american-baptist-history/.

contributions of African Americans to the faithful witness of Baptists. The resolution highlighted key figures who obeyed the Great Commission mandate, "such as George Liele, recognized as the first overseas missionary from the United States in 1782; Lott Carey, a pioneer in organizing African American Missions in the 1800s; S. M. Lockridge, a dedicated preacher of the gospel in the twentieth century; Sid Smith, one of the first African American Southern Baptist denominational leaders in the modern era; and Fred Luter, the first elected African American president of the Southern Baptist Convention in 2012." "Fred Luter's presidency attracted attention from national news and media outlets. Some critics dismissed his election as tokenism, suggesting that the SBC's declining membership led to Luter's presidency."[3] However, I wanted Liberty Hill parishioners to have a closer look at Luter's life and track record within the SBC, which tells a different story.

Fred Luter Jr., born on November 11, 1956, in New Orleans, Louisiana, made history as the first African American president of the SBC, serving from 2012 to 2014. Luter's early life was marked by modest beginnings. He was raised in New Orleans's Lower Ninth Ward alongside his four siblings by their mother, Viola Brooks, who worked as a seamstress and surgical scrub assistant. In 1977, when he was twenty-one, a motorcycle crash resulted in a compound fracture in Luter's left leg and a severe head injury.[4]

---

[3] Jena McGregor, "Southern Baptist Convention Elects Fred Luter as First Black President: What This Leadership Moment Means," *The Washington Post*, June 19, 2012.

[4] McGregor, "Southern Baptist Convention elects Fred Luter as First Black President.

This life-altering event prompted a spiritual reevaluation for Luter, and he began street preaching at the corner of Caffin and Galvez streets in New Orleans. Equipped with a megaphone and the Word of God, Luter sought to capture the attention of those passing by. In 1980, Luter married Elizabeth Williams, and together they welcomed two children into the world. The motorcycle accident, which Luter considers his "Damascus Road experience," played a pivotal role in shaping his spiritual journey and ultimately led him to become a prominent figure within the SBC.[5]

Fred Luter delivered his inaugural sermon in 1983 at New Orleans's Law Street Missionary Baptist Church. Subsequently, he joined the staff of Greater Liberty Baptist Church, and when approached about an opening at Franklin Avenue Baptist Church (FABC), Luter prayerfully considered the opportunity. In 1986, he assumed the role of pastor at Franklin Avenue Baptist Church, a formerly white Southern Baptist congregation in the Ninth Ward of New Orleans that had transitioned into a predominantly black congregation due to white flight. Faced with the imminent threat of closure, the struggling church required effective leadership. Luter's initial strategic move was to implement an evangelism approach aimed at reaching the residents of New Orleans with the gospel. He introduced "FRANgelism," where "FRAN" stands for "Friends, Relatives, Associates, Neighbors."[6] This innovative strategy encouraged parishioners and converts alike to invite their relatives, friends,

---

[5] Laura Hooton. "Highlighting Fred Luter Jr." *Black Past*. November 4, 2012. https://www.blackpast.org/african-american-history/luter-fred-jr-1956/.

[6] Fred Luter interview with the author.

and even coworkers to visit Franklin Avenue, fostering growth and community engagement.

Recognizing the importance of engaging men, especially fathers, Fred Luter initiated events tailored to male interests. One notable example was a pay-per-view television boxing match featuring Thomas Hearns and Sugar Ray Leonard. The success of this event extended beyond the boxing match, fostering trust and connections between Luter and men in the local community. Understanding the significance of reaching men for the benefit of families, Luter continued to organize outreach opportunities. Luter believed that "winning the man to Christ meant winning the family to Christ."[7] Under Luter's leadership, FABC experienced rapid growth, and a new facility was needed to accommodate the expanding congregation. By 2005, FABC had surpassed 7,000 members, establishing itself as the largest SBC church in Louisiana.[8] Hurricane Katrina wreaked havoc on FABC's building in 2005, displacing the congregation across the country. In the aftermath, Fred Luter embarked on a journey to rally support from Southern Baptist churches. His efforts involved seeking mission teams, acquiring resources, and garnering assistance for the church's reconstruction. Luter experienced the embodiment of Christ's love through the tangible support provided by hundreds of church leaders.

To anchor the scattered FABC members, Luter established "Franklinaway churches" with ordained ministers in various cities.

---

[7] Fred Luter interview with the author.

[8] McGregor, "Southern Baptist Convention Elects Fred Luter as First Black President."

Locally, First Baptist Church of New Orleans, which had suffered minimal damages, generously offered space for Franklin Avenue's parishioners to gather for worship. Throughout this challenging period, Luter's preaching played a crucial role in uplifting hearts, offering comfort, and instilling hope. In the face of uncertainty, his sermons provided a stabilizing force during this unstable time until FABC officially reopened in 2008.[9]

Pastor Luter's deep connection to the city of New Orleans and the parishioners of FABC is integral to understanding his profound love for all people. Luter, as an indigenous pastor, wholeheartedly embraces the cultural nuances of New Orleans, participating in events like Mardi Gras and second line parades and relishing in local culinary delights such as red beans and rice. His genuine engagement with congregants before, during, and after services goes beyond a mere attempt to win favor; it reflects the heart of a shepherd seeking to encourage and connect with the members of his flock. These seemingly small gestures, over time, have fostered a sense of community that has attracted generations to join his church. It is this genuine and caring approach that positioned Luter to be elected as the first African American president of the SBC.

As Southern Baptist messengers continued to honor the contributions of African Americans, resolutions were made to commemorate and reemphasize significant events in America. One of these was the **Resolution on the Fiftieth Anniversary of the Civil**

[9] McGregor.

Rights Act—Baltimore, Maryland (2014).[10] The Civil Rights Act played a pivotal role in eliminating racial segregation laws that had long shaped the nation. The SBC messengers expressed "deep regret and repudiation for the nation's history of racial segregation and acknowledged the complicity of Southern Baptists who resisted or opposed efforts to dismantle racial hierarchy in churches and society." The resolution also expressed gratitude to God for the increased racial and ethnic diversity within the SBC and called on all gospel-affirming individuals to strive for a more faithful witness.

The **Resolution on Racial Reconciliation—Columbus, Ohio (2015)** underscored an ongoing commitment and accountability to the Bible.[11] SBC messengers affirmed the relevance of Scripture's depicting the image of God, God's universal love, and Jesus's reconciliation of "people from every tribe, tongue, and nation." This resolution, structured around biblical principles, shifted the conversation on racial reconciliation from a mere moral obligation to a clear biblical mandate. Messengers renewed their dedication to the "holy responsibility and privilege of loving and discipling people of all races and ethnicities." They urged all Southern Baptist churches to manifest their commitment to racial reconciliation by actively seeking "increased racial and ethnic diversity in church staff roles, leadership positions, and church membership." The resolution also called on Southern Baptist entities and convention committees "to

---

[10] "Resolution on Fiftieth Anniversary of the Civil Rights Act," sbc.net, June 1, 2014, https://www.sbc.net/resource-library/resolutions/on-the-fiftieth-anniversary-of-the-civil-rights-act/.

[11] "Resolution on Racial Reconciliation," sbc.net, June 1, 2015, https://www.sbc.net/resource-library/resolutions/on-racial-reconciliation/.

make leadership appointments that mirror the racial and ethnic diversity of the body of Christ and the SBC." As the SBC advanced its efforts toward racial reconciliation, the nation experienced a significant shift that would test the harmony within the convention.

The **Resolution on Sensitivity and Unity Regarding the Confederate Battle Flag—St. Louis, Missouri (2016)** emerged against the backdrop of national tension and violence surrounding Southern symbols.[12] The Confederate flag, once seen by some as a symbol of evil and racism and by others as a representation of history and pride, came under scrutiny. Southern Baptist messengers issued a resolution to mobilize Southern Baptists against the persistence of racism and to "replace these evils with the beauty of grace and love." The resolution was prompted by the tragic events of June 17, 2015, when twenty-one-year-old Dylann Roof entered the Bible study at the Emanuel African Methodist Episcopal Church in Charleston, South Carolina, and killed nine people. The messengers of the SBC recognized the tragic incident as a hate crime and, through this resolution, appealed to its members to cease the display of the Confederate battle flag as an expression of unity within the entire body of Christ. Additionally, the resolution encouraged Southern Baptists to practice sensitivity, ensuring that nothing fosters division or impedes the unity of the body of Christ, and to serve as a courageous testimony to the transformative influence of Jesus. However, dissenting opinions persisted,

---

[12] "Resolution on Sensitivity and Unity Regarding the Confederate Battle Flag," sbc.net, June 1, 2016, https://www.sbc.net/resource-library/resolutions/on-sensitivity-and-unity-regarding-the-confederate-battle-flag/.

leading to further deliberations and responses from messengers in the subsequent year.

In the **Resolution on the Anti-gospel of Alt-right White Supremacy—Phoenix, Arizona (2017),** the SBC messengers explicitly "condemn[ed] and reject[ed] white supremacy and all manifestations of racial and ethnic hatred as a strategy of the devil designed to bring pain and division to our society."[13] They acknowledged the "need to eradicate racism in all its forms and fervently prayed for those who embrace racist ideologies, hoping they would recognize their errors in the light of the gospel, repent of their prejudices, and experience the peace and love of Christ through redeemed fellowship in the Kingdom of God, where people from every nation, tribe, people, and language are united." What takes precedent for the SBC is the gospel message, and the messengers' resolutions reflected that message.

---

[13] "Resolution on the Anti-gospel of Alt-right White Supremacy," sbc.net, June 1, 2017, https://www.sbc.net/resource-library/resolutions/on-the-anti-gospel-of-alt-right-white-supremacy/.

8

Can We Reconnect the Narrative?

As a result of the presentation, Liberty Hill Baptist Church parishioners are now acquainted with the resolutions of the SBC. As the potential for changed hearts lingers, a critical question emerges: Could the information shared in my presentation become a bridge for unity within the SBC? The initial aspiration was that this presentation would inspire parishioners to sustain a longstanding relationship with the members of the SBC, fostering enduring partnerships for the glory of God. Now, the hope is that the information shared serves as a catalyst for unity, understanding, and a shared commitment to the principles of justice, reconciliation, and the teachings of Christ within the SBC.

It is crucial to acknowledge that this narrative goes beyond the confines of a black church or a white convention. Instead, it emphasizes the necessity of individuals from diverse backgrounds uniting to share the glorious gospel of Jesus Christ. The quest for racial reconciliation extends beyond mere camaraderie; it encompasses the collective effort to engage in the work of ministry in unity. The black church discovers strength when intertwined with the white convention, and conversely, the white convention attains strength through its connection with the black church. This reciprocal relationship underscores the importance of mutual connection for the effective execution of the work of ministry. In this symbiotic partnership, neither side can stand alone to confront the challenges presented by the world. Each party requires the other to open doors, provide resources, offer diverse perspectives, share unique gifts, provide guidance, or simply offer support. Together, they can encourage each other through life's challenges and contribute to a more unified and impactful ministry.

The significance of unity becomes increasingly vital as the world grapples with divisiveness and anxieties. Togetherness can form an unbreakable bond, characterized by acts of profound love. Though there are still issues to be addressed, unity within the convention should stand as a powerful witness to the world. An unnamed pastor called me to discuss the ongoing struggle with racial tensions in some church communities. Despite his efforts to promote unity and love for all races, the resistance he faced from church deacons highlighted deep-seated issues. The irony of deacons, originally appointed to address unfair treatment in Acts 6, instead perpetuating unfair treatment, added a layer of complexity. The pastor's removal from his position and subsequent ministry in a multicultural congregation underscores the difficulties in navigating racial tensions within the church. It is a poignant reminder of the ongoing work needed to foster genuine unity and understanding among believers. Being unified is not optional; the body of Christ is called to stand in all things, even if those things are difficult.

Within the expansive SBC, consisting of over 47,000 autonomous churches, a spectrum of perspectives emerges as congregations navigate the challenges posed by evolving demographics. In 1995, the convention took a significant step by issuing an apology, condemning divisive rhetoric, and endorsing African American leadership. However, as the church aimed for progress, a new societal issue entered its realm: critical race theory. As discussions within Southern Baptist circles revisited historical transgressions, they prompted anticipation for a resolution to clarify the convention's overarching stance. In 2019 in Birmingham, Alabama, a gathering of 12,000 attendees, including over 8,000 voting members, dove into concerns raised by some evangelicals over the use of frameworks such as critical race theory and intersectionality.

Characterized as a collection of "analytical tools that explain how race has and continues to function in society," critical race theory, along with intersectionality, defined as "the study of how different personal characteristics overlap and inform one's experience," emerged as a contentious issue nationally. However, within the SBC, messengers denounced these ideologies and methods as the cause for sharp disagreements and pointed to their inherent conflict with God's Word. Whether in concurrence or dissent, the SBC has consistently adhered to the authority and sufficiency of Scripture since its establishment. Messengers within the SBC asserted that these frameworks "alone are insufficient to diagnose and redress the root causes of the social ills that they identify, which result from sin." The resolution, however, recognized them as "analytical tools [that] can aid in evaluating a variety of human experiences."

The SBC messengers reiterated their commitment to racial reconciliation, emphasizing that it is "built upon biblical presuppositions and is committed to seeking biblical justice through biblical means."[1] While this stance may be offensive to non-Christians, Southern Baptists firmly "affirm Scripture as the first, last, and sufficient authority with regard to how the Church seeks to redress social ills. Anything conflicting with Scripture is rejected, and theories such as Critical Race Theory and Intersectionality are viewed as analytical tools subordinate to Scripture." The resolution underscored that "the gospel of Jesus Christ alone grants the power to change people and society."

While members of the SBC acknowledge historical missteps such as slavery, the Civil War, injustices, lynchings, Jim Crow laws, water hoses, police dogs, billy clubs, and segregated circumstances, it is crucial to recognize that beneath the darkness of those times, voices of unity were crying out in the wilderness. Over the years, those voices have grown louder, and SBC resolutions have provided a space for messengers to express concerns, outrage, disappointments, and calls for action. They play a crucial role as a platform for Southern Baptist messengers to advocate for change and uphold a biblical standard. However, the power of these resolutions is magnified when made in unity with brothers and sisters of diverse

---

[1] "Resolution on Critical Race Theory and Intersectionality," sbc.net, June 1, 2019, https://www.sbc.net/resource-library/resolutions/on-critical-race-theory-and-intersectionality/.

backgrounds. Addressing shared concerns collectively fosters a sense of community and collaboration, even if the opposition is within the SBC.

The acknowledgment of the historical belief in the "curse of Ham" underscored the SBC's commitment to address past misconceptions and discriminatory teachings within its member churches.[2] Messengers openly recognized that this doctrine had been historically used "to enslave and continues to be used by white supremacists as a cloak to invoke God's holy name in unholy acts of demeaning, dishonoring, and dehumanizing certain people who bear His image." Understanding the detrimental impact of this doctrine, they asserted that it "distorted the church's witness" and contradicted broader scriptural teachings that affirm "the image of God in all individuals, regardless of gender or ethnicity." In a determined effort to rectify past injustices and confront the misapplication of biblical verses to justify slavery, the SBC messengers directly addressed this issue. While the resolution may seem matter-of-fact, its significance lies in the convention's commitment to racial reconciliation and its resolve to correct historical wrongs associated with misinterpretations of Scripture.

The resolution also recognized the Ethics and Religious Liberty Commission's acknowledgment of the "fiftieth anniversary of the assassination of Rev. Dr. Martin Luther King Jr. that occurred on April 4, 1968, in Memphis, Tennessee." It provided

[2] "Resolution on Renouncing the Doctrine of the 'curse of Ham' as a Justification for Racism," sbc.net, June 1, 2018, https://www.sbc.net/resource-library/resolutions/on-renouncing-the-doctrine-of-the-curse-of-ham-as-a-justification-for-racism/.

a platform for introspection, "repentance, and a renewed commitment toward racial harmony." With unanimous backing and no public dissent, the messengers reaffirmed their unwavering stance against racism in all its manifestations, expressly rejecting the "curse of Ham" doctrine and any other efforts to manipulate or misinterpret the Bible to justify injustices. Furthermore, the resolution earnestly implored divine intervention, seeking God's purification of hearts and the "healing and restoration of individuals affected by this sort of doctrine." It emphasized a steadfast commitment to "forestall any recurrence of this pernicious teaching from infiltrating hearts or pulpits."

As this book ends, the answers to the questions presented are worth addressing. **Can we retell the story? We must retell the story!** The history of black-white relationships has, unfortunately, divided us mentally, physically, emotionally, and spiritually. Many have become accustomed to living in their own separate worlds, missing out on the valuable lessons that come from shared life experiences. The fear of the "other" has erected invisible fences that hinder integration. Yet there is a narrative to be recounted—one that is not a fairy tale or even suitable for a PG-13 rating. It is a story steeped in blood, a constant reminder of the hurdles that must be overcome for unity and equality. However, the cross of Jesus Christ is an integral part of this story, at times bearing abuse like that faced by the marginalized. The Bible itself became weaponized, leading people to reject its essence of purity and love. Yet within the pages of the Bible lies a greater narrative, offering a pathway beyond the evils of humanity. It is a story that lifts the brokenhearted and sets the captives free. We must retell the story of a Savior who enters into the broken pages of our lives and rewrites our story with unity and love.

Can we release the hurt? Indeed, we must release the hurt! The African American story is indelible, woven into the very fabric of the earth's foundations, preordained with the strength to overcome atrocities, stand victorious in the face of obstacles, and endure injustices. Despite the multifaceted hurt—be it mental, physical, psychological, or spiritual—African Americans are not destined to be hostages of the past. Releasing the hurt grants permission to soar above the story of slavery and injustice. As believers, we must intentionally release our hurt, paving the way for others to release their hurts. It becomes a purposeful endeavor to experience freedom and, in turn, facilitate the freedom of others.

Can we reestablish trust? Indeed, we must be willing to reestablish trust, even while acknowledging the potential for disappointment or mistreatment. The prospect of racial reconciliation hinges on the restoration of trust. The pivotal question becomes, Whom do we trust with the most intimate details of our lives? Humanity, despite its best intentions, often falls short of keeping promises. Families may let us down, and despite our earnest desire to love, the risk of losing trust remains inevitable. However, there is One who is truly worthy of our deepest trust, and he alone can be trusted with the intimate details of our lives. In case you have not realized it, that One is Jesus Christ, our trustworthy source.

Can we reduce the noise? Yes, we must deliberately reduce the noise! The cacophony of the world rages like the mighty sea. World news and online updates can pull people into a tailspin as they grapple with the evils of humanity. Death tolls rise and violence fills the earth with heinous crimes. The volume gets louder and louder, making it challenging for the mind to find rest. Police brutality, racial discrimination, and various interferences hinder us from quieting our minds and hearts to tune in to what the Lord may be communicating. Do not be deceived; the volume can be diminished by taking all your burdens to the Lord in prayer. The sounds are the enemy's distractions aiming to prevent unity. However, if Christians of all ethnicities increasingly realize all that we have in common, the noise will decrease, and our ability to hear from our Lord will increase and provide direction.

Can we regain the courage? Yes, we must regain our courage! Long gone are the days of sitting on the sidelines and cheering from the stands. Racial reconciliation requires participants who are willing to suit up and get in the game. The day is coming when Christians will be unable to hide behind their pulpits, choir robes, worship bands, Sunday school classes, community groups, mission trips, or church doors. Faith will no longer be defined by what you believe but by what you do in moments of controversy. Are you the kind of Christian who will acquiesce in order to keep peace and avoid causing problems in your selected group, or will you stand on what you believe and do the will of God? Having the courage to stand for God requires the belief that God will see you through, no matter how difficult, no matter how lonely, and no matter how hard the task may be. We must be strong in the Lord and in the power of his might.

Can we rediscover the cross? Yes, we must rediscover the cross! At the cross, we have the blueprint for reconciliation. On the cross, Jesus provided everything needed for unity and hope.

At the cross, there is no pity party about what happened to any individual because the sole focus is on Jesus and how he responds to the tragic events of his life. The cross is a picture of love, and though the standard set by Jesus is high, he also provides everything that we need to meet the standard and offers redemption, peace, joy, and reconciliation.

Can we reclaim the mission? Yes, we must reclaim the mission. The Great Commission is more than a memory verse; it is a source of strength and direction as we shift our focus from ourselves to others. The Great Commission refuses to let believers internalize what is happening individually but instead directs our attention toward sinners, providing an opportunity to have eternal life in Christ. "Go, get, guide, grow, go"—this is how we unify to reclaim the mission. First, the Great Commission instructs believers to "go," meaning we must not remain where we are. The second step, "get," does not specify the type of encounter but implies that we must interact with someone else. Third, we are to "guide," which involves teaching unbelievers the lessons of the gospel in both word and deed. The fourth step in this teaching process, "grow," includes a fellowship component that allows unbelievers to observe all things Jesus commanded. The last step is "go," which in turn puts them on the cycle of doing the exact same thing. Reclaiming the mission requires diligence, openness, and a willingness to go the extra mile with and for someone else.

Can we reshape that narrative? Yes, we must reshape the narrative! This narrative involves a united front pushing back the darkness in the world. Divisiveness remains a trick of the enemy, hindering the body of believers from coming together to fulfill

God's purposes. We must reshape the narrative, prioritizing the new over the old. The old narrative emphasizes pain, dysfunction, and separation. However, a new narrative can emphasize joy, unity, and togetherness, essential for achieving the purposes God has set before us. If believers unite, the world can witness hope in Christ and experience a peace that surpasses understanding. Let us reshape the narrative and accomplish God's purposes together.

BIBLIOGRAPHY

"African-American Missions." *The Traveling Team*. Last modified February 11, 2015. https://www.thetravelingteam.org/articles /african-american-missions.

"Civil Rights Act of 1866, 'An Act to Protect All Persons in the United States in Their Civil Rights, and Furnish the Means of Their Vindication.'" National Constitution Center. Accessed July 16, 2024. https://constitution center .org/the-constitution/historic-document-library/detail/civil -rights-act-of-1866-april-9-1866-an-act-to-protect-all -persons-in-the-united-states-in-their-civil-rights-and-furnish -the-means-of-their-vindication.

Dart, John. "Southern Baptists Vote to Issue Apology for Past Racism." *The Los Angeles Times*. June 21, 1995. https://www.la times.com/archives/la-xpm-1995-06-21-mn-15534-story.html.

Fletcher, Jesse C. *Southern Baptist Convention: A Sesquicentennial History*. Nashville: B&H, 1994.

Florido, Adrian. "How Black Activists Used Lynching Souvenirs to Expose American Violence." NPR, February 8, 2022. https://

www.npr.org/2022/02/08/1078977454/race-racism-lynching-postcards-ahmaud-arbery-george-floyd.

Forliti, Amy. "Prosecutors: Officer Was on Floyd's Neck for about 9 Minutes." *AP News*. Last modified March 4, 2021. https://apnews.com/article/trials-derek-chauvin-minneapolis-racial-injustice-060f6e9e8b7079505 a1b096a68311c2b.

Hagerty, Barbara Bradley. "Southern Baptists See Their Future in a Black Pastor." NPR, June 19, 2012. https://www.npr.org/2012/06/19/155123446/southern-baptists-see-their-future-in-a-black-pastor.

"Hillyer Resolutions." sbc.net. Accessed July 16, 2024. https://www.sbc.net/resource-library/resolutions/hillyer-resolutions/.

"John F. Kennedy and Religion." John F. Kennedy Presidential Library and Museum. Accessed July 17, 2024. https://www.jfklibrary.org/learn/about-jfk/jfk-in-history/john-f-kennedy-and-religion.

"Lynching: Florida's Brutal Distinction." *Orlando Sentinel*, March 7, 1993. Accessed July 16, 2024. https://www.orlandosentinel.com/1993/03/07/lynching-floridas-brutal-distinction/.

"'137 Shots' Documentary Explores Fatal Shooting of Timothy Russell and Malissa Williams Debuts Wed." *News 5 Cleveland WEWS*. Last modified December 15, 2021. https://www.news5cleveland.com/news/137-shots/137-shots-documentary-explores-fatal-shooting-of-timothy-russell-and-malissa-williams-debuts-wed.

"On Renouncing the Doctrine of the 'Curse of Ham' as a Justification for Racism." sbc.net. Accessed July 16, 2024. https://www.sbc.net/resource-library/resolutions/on-renouncing

-the-doctrine-of-the-curse-of-ham-as-a-justification-for-racism/.

"Recommendation on Law and Order." sbc.net. Accessed July 16, 2024. https://www.sbc.net/resource-library/resolutions/recommendation-on-law-and-order/.

"Resolution Concerning Lynching and Race Relations." sbc.net. Accessed July 16, 2024. https://www.sbc.net/resource-library/resolutions/resolution-concerning-lynching-and-race-relations/.

"Resolution on Cooperation with Other Baptists." sbc.net. Accessed July 16, 2024. https://www.sbc.net/resource-library/resolutions/resolution-on-cooperation-with-other-baptists-13/.

"Resolution on Lynching on Mob Violence." sbc.net. Accessed July 16, 2024. https://www.sbc.net/resource-library/resolutions/resolution-on-lynching-on-mob-violence/.

Silverstein, Jason. "The Global Impact of George Floyd: How Black Lives Matter Protests Shaped Movements around the World." *CBS News*. Last modified June 4, 2021. https://www.cbsnews.com/news/george-floyd-black-lives-matter-impact/.

Torbet, Robert G. *History of the Baptists*. 3rd ed. Valley Forge, PA: Judson Press, 1973.

Williams, Jarvis J., and Kevin M. Jones. *Removing the Stain of Racism from the Southern Baptist Convention: Diverse African American and White Perspectives*. Nashville: B&H Academic, 2017.

GENERAL INDEX

L

M

N

P

R

SCRIPTURE INDEX